THE KINGFISHER
Young People's
Pocket
Atlas

KINGFISHER
Larousse Kingfisher Chambers Inc.
95 Madison Avenue
New York, New York 10016

First edition 1997

2 4 6 8 10 9 7 5 3

LIBRARY OF CONGRESS CATALOGING-IN-PUBLICATION DATA
Has been applied for
ISBN 0-7534-5064-X

Produced by Miles Kelly Publishing Ltd.
Designer: Smiljka Surla
Editors: Rosie Alexander, Samantha Armstrong,
  Angela Royston
Assistant Editor: Susanne Bull
Picture Research: Kate Miles, Yannick Yago

Printed in Hong Kong

THE KINGFISHER
Young People's
Pocket
Atlas

Linda Sonntag

Kingfisher

NEW YORK

CONTENTS

4 **Contents**

5 **Introduction**
6 Planet Earth
8 The Solar System
10 World facts and figures
12 How maps are made
14 Environment
16 Population
18 Government
20 Religion

22 **North America**
24 Canada
28 United States
34 Central America and
the Caribbean

40 **South America**
42 The Andean States
46 Brazil and its neighbors
50 The Southern States

54 **Europe**
56 Scandinavia and Finland
60 Netherlands, Belgium,
and Luxembourg
64 The British Isles
68 Germany
72 Switzerland, Austria,
and Liechtenstein
76 France
80 Spain and Portugal
84 Italy and its neighbors
88 Poland and its neighbors
92 The Balkans and Romania

96 **Russia and its neighbors**

108 **Asia**
110 China and its neighbors
116 Japan
120 Southeast Asia
124 India and its neighbors
130 The Middle East

136 **Africa**
138 North Africa
144 West Africa
148 Central and East Africa
154 Southern Africa

158 **Australasia**
160 The Pacific Islands
166 New Zealand
170 Australia

174 Antarctica
176 The Arctic

178 **Glossary**
184 **Index**
191 **Acknowledgments**

INTRODUCTION

W e live in a changing world. Major wars can cause some countries to change their boundaries or even disappear altogether, and new countries to be created. Political events also change the world map. In the 1950s and 1960s, many colonies in Africa and Asia became independent and adopted new names. Another period of massive change occurred during the late 1980s and early 1990s, when the formerly communist Soviet Union changed its policies and decided to break up into 15 separate countries. Around the same time, in eastern Europe, the former communist Federal People's Republic of Yugoslavia split into five countries, while Czechoslovakia was divided into two.

The Pocket Atlas is an essential tool for anyone who wants to study and understand the changing world of the late 1990s. It contains maps that show new countries, including those in eastern Europe and the former Soviet Union. There is also information on the geography and history of countries, together with descriptions of how the peoples of the world live and work. The Atlas begins with a reference section on planet Earth that covers its evolution and life today. The main body of the book contains chapters on the six populated continents and the countries they contain. There is also a special section on Russia and its neighbors, which explains how the former Soviet Union split apart into 15 republics. One of them is Russia, the world's largest country, which lies partly in Europe and partly in Asia. Of the 14 other republics, six are in Europe and eight are in Asia. At the back of the Atlas is a chapter on the icy polar regions and a glossary of technical terms.

The peoples of the world

There are thousands of cultures in the world today, each with its own language. This is what makes the world such a diverse and exciting place in which to live.

Planet Earth

Most scientists believe that the Sun, Earth, and other planets formed about 4.6 billion years ago from a huge cloud of tiny solid particles and gases called a nebula. The solid particles and some of the gas had been thrown out of earlier stars that had died. The nebula began to shrink and spin, collapsing inwards because of its own gravity. Soon, material near the center was colliding at tremendous speeds and giving out so much heat that a glowing star, the Sun, was born. The rest of the nebula formed into a ring around the Sun and collisions inside this ring built up the planets, including our own planet Earth.

For a time the planets were very hot, but they never became hot enough to shine like stars. All the planets were bombarded by other much smaller bodies, so that their surfaces became covered with craters like the ones still seen on the Moon today. On the Earth, however, wind and rain have gradually worn most of the craters away.

Buried deep in the heart of our planet is a metal core of iron and nickel that is larger than the Moon and almost as hot as the surface of the Sun. The outer layer of the core is liquid metal, but enormous pressure at the center has compressed it into a solid. When Earth formed 4.6 billion years ago, it glowed red hot and the molten metals sank to its center while the lighter rocks floated to the surface.

Around the core is wrapped a thick layer of hot rock called the mantle. This acts like a heated blanket, holding in the warmth. Around the mantle is a third layer called the crust, which forms the rocky surface of the Earth on which we live. The thickest parts of the crust are about 35 miles deep, but if the Earth were compared to an apple, the crust would be only as thick as the apple's skin.

The mantle contains traces of radioactive uranium which steadily gives out heat. This warmth rises, creating a more fluid part of the mantle known as the asthenosphere. Above the

---

■ EARTH FACTS

Diameter at the equator:
  7,926 miles
Diameter at the poles: 7,900 miles
Diameter of core: 4,340 miles
Thickness of mantle: 1,800 miles
Temperature of inner core:
  up to 13,000° F
Mass: 6.6 sextillion tons
Average density: 363 lb / square foot
Land area: 57 million square miles
Ocean area: 139 million square miles
Volume of ocean:
  1,314 million cubic miles
Age: 4.6 billion years
Atmosphere: 78% nitrogen,
  21% oxygen, 1% argon
Time to rotate on axis:
  23 hours 56 minutes
Time to orbit the Sun:
  About 365 days 6 hours

partly fluid asthenosphere lies the lithosphere, which includes the outermost mantle and the crust. The lithosphere is made up of massive plates that float on the asthenosphere. These plates are constantly moving, causing the continents to drift apart, mountains to form, the ground to shake, and volcanoes to erupt.

The continents reached their present positions around 50 million years ago (mya) and are still slowly drifting as the planet evolves. The Himalayas began to form 40 mya, and continue to be built up and worn gradually away.

Life probably began about 3.5 billion years ago in muddy puddles or along the shores of shallow lakes. Lightning and radiation may have built up simple organic molecules that combined with clay particles to form the first cells. The first living things were microscopic bacteria and algae that grew in large mats by the tide line.

Earth's original atmosphere probably contained large amounts of carbon dioxide, a gas made up of carbon and oxygen. The earliest plants used the carbon dioxide to make food and released the oxygen on which all animal life depends. The first animals were jellyfish-like creatures. The first mammals appeared 216 mya, but the first humans did not walk the Earth for another 214 million years.

The Sun will shine for millions more years, but then it will burn up all its fuel and die. The Earth will be left as a cold, lifeless rock.

Outer core
A strongly magnetic mass of molten metal

Mantle
Hot rock making up most of the Earth

Asthenosphere
The hot and fluid part of the mantle

Lithosphere
The cool crust and upper mantle

Inner core
A very hot solid mix of iron and nickel

Crust
The Earth's rocky skin

The Solar System

T he Earth belongs to a family of nine planets, each of which is in orbit (circling) around the Sun. Together they make up the Solar System, which also includes the moons orbiting around their planets, lumps of rock called asteroids, and comets with their long tails of dust and gas.

The Sun, the star at the center of the Solar System, is a burning hot ball of shining gas. Without its heat and light the Earth would be a frozen dead world. Among the nine planets that orbit the Sun, the Earth is unique. Only the Earth has water in its oceans and enough oxygen to support animal life. Mercury, Venus, Mars, and Pluto are rocky wastes. The giant planets Jupiter, Saturn, Uranus, and Neptune are globes of gas and ice particles. The Earth is habitable because it is at just the right distance from the Sun. A little closer and it would resemble scorching Venus.

A little farther away and it would be a permanently frozen waste.

However, the Earth has not always been as it is now. Soon after it formed, about 4.6 billion years ago, this planet was a roasting cauldron. Over millions of years the surface cooled and the atmosphere, oceans, and continents formed.

Life began in the still, tropically warm oceans about 3.5 billion years ago with microscopic life forms. Many scientists believe that the first animals and plants began to develop and live on land about 400 million years ago.

Mercury

Earth

Venus

Sun

Mars

Jupiter

Outside our Solar System are other solar systems that have developed around other stars as hot as our Sun. Many scientists believe that intelligent life must exist on other planets like our Earth. Some scientists hope to find other inhabited planets by picking up radio signals sent out by any alien civilizations that may exist. A project called the Search for Extra-Terrestrial Intelligence (SETI) has been trying to identify signals from space that sound artificial. So far it has been unsuccessful.

Other scientists have sent out radio messages from Earth in the hope of a reply. Some space probes have plaques on their sides showing the position of Earth. Others have electronically encoded pictures, greetings and music. It is hoped that as they drift out of our Solar System and into others, alien spacecraft may intercept them because they want to find out about life on other planets such as ours.

Pluto

Neptune

Uranus

Saturn

■ **EARTH FACTS**
Circumference around the equator:
24,902 miles
Circumference around the poles:
24,860 miles
Distance to the center of the Earth:
About 3,950 miles
Surface area:
About 196,800,000 square miles
Average distance from the Moon:
238,700 miles
Average distance from the Sun:
92,752,000 miles
Rotation speed: 1,030 mph at
the equator
Speed in orbit: 18.5 miles per second
Chief elements of the Earth's crust:
Oxygen (46.6%), silicon (27.7%),
aluminum (8.1%), iron (5%)

9

World facts and figures

The surface of the Earth is about 70 percent water and 30 percent land. The largest ocean is the Pacific, which is larger than all the land put together. Asia is the largest continent. It covers nearly a third of the total land area.

■ **EARTH EXTREMES**

Hottest shade temperature recorded: 135.9° F at Al'Aziziyah, Libya, on 9.13.22

Coldest temperature recorded: -129.9° F at Vostock, Antarctica, on 7.21.83

Highest annual rainfall: 463 inches at Tutunendo, Colombia

Most rain in one month: 366 inches at Cherrapunji, India, in July 1861

Driest place on Earth: no rain, near Calama, Atacama Desert, Chile

Most snow in one year: 1,224 inches on Mt. Rainier, Washington State, 1971–1972

Greatest tides: 53.5 feet in Bay of Fundy, Nova Scotia, Canada

Strongest surface wind recorded: 281 mph at Mt. Washington, New Hampshire, 1934

Greatest ocean depth: 36,197 feet, Marianas Trench, Pacific Ocean

Deepest gorge: 7,874 feet, Hells Canyon, Idaho

Longest gorge: 216 miles, Grand Canyon, Arizona

Highest navigated lake: Titicaca, Peru/Bolivia, 12,503 feet above sea level

Deepest lake: Baikal, Siberia, Russia, 6,365 feet

■ **OCEANS**
Pacific, 69,600,000 sq. mi.
Atlantic, 40,750,000 sq. mi.
Indian, 28,250,000 sq. mi.
Arctic, 5,516,000 sq. mi.

■ **LONGEST RIVERS**
Nile, Africa, 4,135 miles
Amazon, S. America, 3,998 miles
Mississippi-Missouri-Red Rock, N. America, 3,863 miles
Yenisey, Russia, 3,435 miles
Chang Jiang, China, 3,391 miles
Ob-Irtysh, Russia, 3,193 miles
Lena, Russia, 2,993 miles
Zaire, Africa, 2,993 miles
Amur, Asia, 2,794 miles
Huang He, China, 2,694 miles
Mekong, S.E. Asia, 2,594 miles
Niger, Africa, 2,594 miles

Traditional feluccas sail on the Nile River.

■ **DESERTS**
Sahara, 3,229,000 sq. mi.
Australian Desert, 595,800 sq. mi.
Arabian Desert, 500,000 sq. mi.
Gobi, 400,000 sq. mi.
Kalahari, 200,000 sq. mi.

Sand dunes are shaped by desert winds.

■ MAJOR WATERFALLS

Highest: Angel Falls, Venezuela,
3,212 feet
Tugela Falls, South Africa, 3,110 feet
Yosemite Falls, California, 2,425 feet
Greatest volume: Boyoma Falls,
Zaire, 567,000 cu. ft./sec.
Niagara, N. America, 200,000 cu.
ft./sec.

*Adventurers bungee-jump off
Angel Falls.*

■ LARGEST ISLANDS

Greenland, N. Atlantic,
836,300 sq. mi.
New Guinea, S.W. Pacific,
305,248 sq. mi.
Borneo, S.W. Pacific, 288,714 sq. mi.
Madagascar, Indian Ocean,
225,660 sq. mi.
Baffin Island, Canadian Arctic,
183,000 sq. mi.
Sumatra, Indian Ocean,
166,054 sq. mi.
Honshu, N.W. Pacific,
88,728 sq. mi.
Great Britain, N. Atlantic,
88,229 sq. mi.
Ellesmere Island, Canadian Arctic,
76,262 sq. mi.
Victoria Island, Canadian Arctic,
74,072 sq. mi.

■ HIGHEST MOUNTAINS

Asia: Everest, Himalayas – Nepal,
29,028 feet
K2 (Godwin Austen), Karakoram,
China/Pakistan/India, 28,251 feet
Kanchenjunga, Himalayas – Nepal,
28,208 feet
Makalu, Himalayas – Nepal, 27,789
feet
Dhaulagiri, Himalayas – Nepal,
26,811 feet
Nanga Parbat, Himalayas – India,
26,660 feet
Annapurna, Himalayas – Nepal,
26,493 feet
South America: Aconcagua, Andes –
Argentina, 22,835 feet
North America: Denali (McKinley),
Alaska – 20,322 feet
Africa: Kilimanjaro – Tanzania,
19,340 feet
Europe: Elbrus, Caucasus – Russia,
18,481 feet
Mont Blanc, Alps – France,
15,771 feet
Antarctica: Vinson Massif,
16,864 feet
Australasia: Wilhelm, Bismarck –
New Guinea, 15,400 feet

*Snow covers the summit of
Mount Everest.*

How maps are made

The oldest surviving maps were made by the Babylonians, who lived in modern-day Iraq more than 4,000 years ago. Many ancient mapmakers thought that the Earth was flat, but the first sea voyages around the world in the 1600s led to a great improvement in the accuracy of mapmaking.

The only really accurate map of the world is a globe, which is round like the Earth itself. Mapmakers use a technique called projection to show the curved surface of the Earth on flat maps of continents and countries. It is impossible for all areas, shapes, distances, and directions to be drawn accurately on a flat map, so map projections are worked out mathematically to preserve chosen features. For example, Mercator's projection distorts areas in order to maintain directions, so that it can be used for navigation.

Mapmakers drew imaginary lines around the Earth in a grid to help the mapreader find places. These are lines of latitude and longitude. Lines of latitude run horizontally across the globe. The line where the Earth's circumference is at its greatest is called the equator. Parallel lines of latitude are drawn north and south of the equator.

Lines of longitude divide the Earth up through its poles, like the segments of an orange. Each line is a great circle going right around the Earth. Lines of longitude have no obvious reference point, such as the equator, so English navigators made their home port, Greenwich, on the Thames River near London, the line of zero degrees longitude. Longitude is still measured east and west of this prime meridian.

Early navigators used the stars to find out their position. Latitude was calculated from the heights of the stars in the sky or the position of the Sun as it rose,

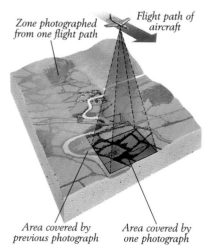

Zone photographed from one flight path

Flight path of aircraft

Area covered by previous photograph

Area covered by one photograph

Maps from aerial photographs

Aerial photographs were first used for map making during World War I. Modern aerial photographs are taken with a 60% overlap. When pairs of photographs are viewed stereoscopically, the land appears in 3D and contours can be plotted.

set or reached its zenith (highest point). Longitude can also be measured against the stars, but it is necessary to know the exact time, because the stars move east to west across the sky. In the mid-1700s an English navigator, John Harrison, invented an instrument called the marine chronometer. This made it possible to measure longitude accurately, so that more accurate maps could be made. By comparing local time, measured from the angle of the Sun, with Greenwich mean time on the chronometer, the navigator could work out how far east or west he was from the prime meridian.

Mercator's projection (cylindrical)

Conical projection

Zenithal or azimuthal projection

Peters' projection (equal area)

Goode's projection (interrupted equal area)

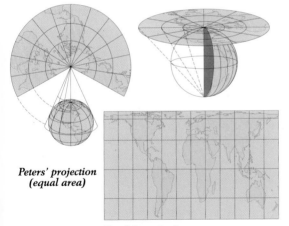

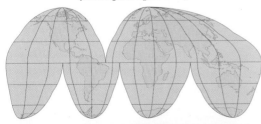

Map projections
. . . .
The principle of Mercator's projection is shown by wrapping a piece of paper around the equator to form a cylinder. The landmasses have the right shape, but are stretched toward the poles. In Peters' projection landmasses have correct areas, but their shape is squashed.

In a zenithal projection the paper remains flat and touches the globe at one pole, so that lines of longitude show their correct angles. A conical projection, in which the paper is rolled into a cone and placed over the globe to touch it along one line of latitude, shows countries with the minimum distortion. In Goode's projection the oceans have been opened up to show the continents. No projection is fully accurate. The globe is the only truly accurate world map.

Environment

The environment is the surroundings in which we live. Some parts of it are living, such as plants, animals, and people, while other parts are nonliving, such as air and water. All these elements work together to keep life going.

People have always had an effect on the environment, but today human activities are causing serious damage. The air is being polluted with harmful gases from vehicles and factories. Water is polluted with pesticides, industrial waste and domestic sewage. Forests are cut down for timber and to make way for farmland, which is causing many plants and animals to die out.

Air pollution can damage the Earth's atmosphere and affect the climate. Chemicals called chlorofluorocarbons (CFCs) are destroying the ozone layer, a protective barrier around the Earth that keeps out harmful

Deforestation

When trees are cleared from high ground rainwater rushes downhill, taking soil with it. It floods the ground below and causes rivers to silt up. In the dry season the soil bakes hard and cracks.

radiation from the Sun. Pollution from burning coal, oil and car exhausts increases the greenhouse effect, a process that traps heat from the Sun to warm the Earth. Many scientists believe that this pollution is already making the Earth warmer. If the overall temperature of the world rose by just three degrees, the ice caps at the North and South Poles would melt, causing sea levels to rise and flood many areas.

Habitat destruction is the greatest threat to plant and animal species worldwide. Sometimes forests are cleared to make way for agriculture or housing. However, forests are

Oil spills

Many people volunteer to help animals in danger. If there is an oil spill, the lives of thousands of animals and birds may be at risk. Teams work hard to clean them so that they can be returned to the wild.

vitally important to the environment as a whole. They act as a water-holding system. Without them rivers run faster in rainy seasons, causing soil erosion in their upper reaches and problems of silting as the river approaches the sea. In many areas erosion is robbing the land of nutrients so that deserts continue to spread.

Coral reefs, mangrove swamps, and the entire wetland ecosystem—rivers, streams, lakes, ponds, and marshes—are also under threat. Many types of wildlife are being lost as dams are built to produce power, marshes drained for agricultural land, and tropical swamps cleared for shrimp farms. Surviving wetlands are often damaged by engineering schemes, by pollution from industrial waste, or by thermal pollution from water used for cooling. Another problem is eutrophication. This occurs when nutrients from chemical fertilizers flow off the land and cause ponds and rivers to be choked by a huge growth of weeds.

Governments are being urged to find ways of reducing pollution and conserving the environment to prevent irreparable damage. However, economic and political considerations are often put first. The safety of the planet and of human life is often ignored. The worst ever nuclear accident, in 1986 at Chernobyl, Ukraine, frightened the world. But even the regular disposal of nuclear waste from power stations remains a major problem. Nuclear waste can remain lethal (deadly) for thousands of years and no one yet knows how or where to dispose of it safely and permanently.

Traffic pollution
. . . .
This baby in its stroller is directly exposed to traffic exhaust. Exhaust fumes cause severe breathing problems and can be lethal. Governments are looking at new ways of reducing traffic pollution.

Recycling
. . . .
Every household can save energy, time, and raw resources by recycling some of its waste, including newspapers, glass, and cans. These materials can be broken down and used again.

15

Population

There are well over 5.6 billion people living in the world today and the number is expected to grow to over 9 billion by 2050. Some parts have far more people than others. These are mostly regions where there is fertile agricultural land, such as China, or where big industrial cities have grown up, as has happened in many European countries. From time to time populations change in size.

North America

South America

These tables compare countries by area and population. If population growth is not controlled, some countries may face serious problems in feeding and caring for their people.

■ **LARGEST COUNTRIES BY AREA**
Russia: 6,563,784 sq. mi.
Canada: 3,832,702 sq. mi.
China: 3,679,822 sq. mi.
United States: 3,602,816 sq. mi.
Brazil: 3,272,013 sq. mi.
Australia: 2,965,017 sq. mi.
India: 1,263,715 sq. mi.
Argentina: 1,103,263 sq. mi.
Kazakhstan: 1,044,530 sq. mi.
Sudan: 963,235 sq. mi.

■ **LARGEST COUNTRIES BY POPULATION**
China: 1,205,181,000
India: 913,600,000
United States: 260,529,000
Indonesia: 198,070,000
Brazil: 159,143,000
Russia: 148,366,000
Pakistan: 126,284,000
Japan: 124,959,000
Bangladesh: 122,210,000
Nigeria: 119,328,000

War, drought, famine, and disease may kill huge numbers of people or drive them from their homes. Poverty can force whole communities to move elsewhere in search of a better life.

Populations also grow at different rates. Most Europeans and North Americans are now living longer than ever before because they have good supplies of food and healthcare. However, most of these people are choosing to have fewer children, so the population is growing very slowly. By contrast, in Africa, South America, and Asia, the population is growing rapidly. Many people there lack good food, clean water, medical care, and sanitation. These problems may become even worse if population growth is not controlled. In China strict legislation limits the number of children a woman may have.

The World Health Organization (WHO), which is

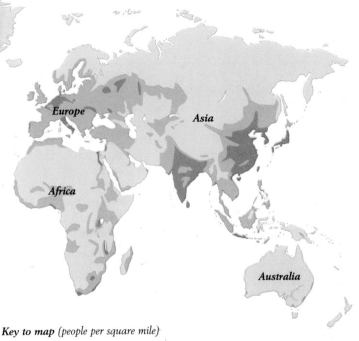

Key to map *(people per square mile)*

■ *over 40* ■ *4-40* □ *less than 4*

part of the United Nations, aims to improve standards of health and health education around the world. The WHO works with governments to provide safe drinking water and adequate sewage disposal. Vaccination programs are now carried out in most countries. Eighty percent of the world's children are now immunized against the killer diseases of polio, tuberculosis, measles, diphtheria, tetanus, and whooping cough.

Most of the world's governments carry out population surveys called censuses, which not only count the number of people, but also record where they live and what sort of job they do. These statistics help countries to measure changes in population and plan for the future.

Key to chart

□ ***Asia*** *3.38 billion*
■ ***Africa*** *697 million*
■ ***Europe*** *(including Russia)* *733 million*
■ ***North and Central America*** *449 million*
■ ***South America*** *316 million*
□ ***Oceania*** *28 million*

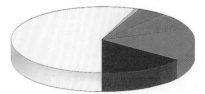

Government

All countries have governments that decide how the country is run. They make laws, set taxes, and spend public money on projects and services of national importance, such as education and defense. Governments have the power to go to war against other countries, although sometimes their decisions may be challenged or changed by public opinion. Governments also have the power to make agreements with other governments. A typical example of this is a trade agreement where countries benefit from selling goods to one another. They can also impose sanctions (economic restrictions) on other governments by either banning trade or taxing imports.

Today most countries are democratic republics. This means the people have elected their government from a choice of political parties and have also elected their head of state. The opposite of a democracy is a dictatorship, a form of government in which one person or a small group of people has absolute power. In a dictatorship there are no elections and people are not free to choose a political party to support. Dictatorships are often run by the army or a monarch.

Communist countries are usually run by one political party, the Communist Party, which believes that everyone should have equal shares in the country's property and wealth, and all jobs should be equal. In communist

United Nations

The General Assembly of the United Nations (UN) meets in New York. The UN works toward world peace.

The Berlin Wall

Germans celebrate becoming one nation again by demolishing the Berlin Wall on October 3, 1990. Germany was divided from 1945 to 1990 into East and West.

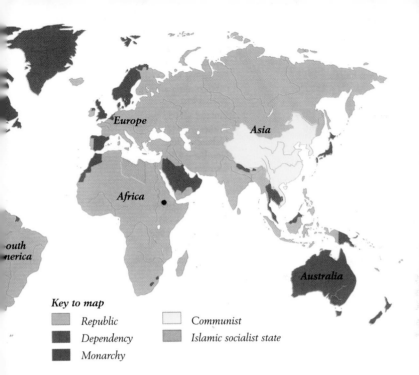

Key to map

- Republic
- Dependency
- Monarchy
- Communist
- Islamic socialist state

countries the economy is directed by the state, which owns and runs businesses, industries, and farms. Private enterprise, in which individuals and groups own and run their own businesses, is not allowed.

A free market is the opposite of a communist economy. This is an economic system that is not directed by the state, and which encourages private enterprise. States that have both public and private ownership are said to have a mixed economy.

Most of the world's governments send representatives to the United Nations (UN) in New York. The UN helps the countries of the world to keep in touch with one another.

■ **TERMS**

These are some of the terms used to describe the way a country is governed.

Monarchy: A country where the head of the state is a monarch (a king or a queen). In a modern constitutional monarchy the monarch's power to govern is strictly limited.

Republic: The opposite of a monarchy, in which the country's head of state is often an elected president.

Democracy: Any form of government that is elected by popular vote. In a democracy voters choose between two or more political parties.

Federal state: The power in federal states is divided between one central and several regional governments.

Dependency: A state ruled by another country.

19

⬤Religion

Since prehistoric times, people everywhere have tried to make sense of the world around them. This search for a meaning to life grew into religious belief. The first religions were based on the worship of natural forces, such as air, fire, and wind, or animals, mountains and rivers. These became linked to powerful supernatural beings—gods and goddesses, spirits and demons.

The Greeks worshipped a mother goddess, patron of fertility and the harvest whom they called Hera. Her consort was Zeus, most powerful of all the gods, and their home was Mount Olympus, the highest peak in Greece. Beyond Olympus was the underworld (the realm of the dead), which was ruled by Hades and his consort Persephone. Roman religion gave the Greek gods

Jerusalem, Israel

Orthodox Jews stand at prayer by Jerusalem's western wall, a holy place called the Wailing Wall.

different names. In addition, every household had its guardian spirits, called the lares and penates, and each person had their own protective spirit or genius.

Today some religions, such as Hinduism, have many gods. Others, such as Islam, Judaism, and Christianity, have only one god. The Chinese religion of Confucianism has no gods at all.

Many religions have developed from older faiths. Christianity sprang from Judaism. Religions are often divided into different groups whose members believe in the same principles, but may interpret them in different ways. Christianity, for example, includes Protestant, Roman Catholic, and Eastern Orthodox groups.

Religion has played a major role in shaping world history and remains a powerful force. Today there are hundreds of religions. Although they may differ widely, they all teach their followers to live by a moral code, which means knowing the difference between right and wrong.

Worship

This chart shows how people worshiped at the beginning of the 1990s. The largest group is Christian, followed by Muslim and Hindu.

- Christian 33.5%
- No religion 20.7%
- Muslim 18.2%
- Hindu 13.5%
- Other 7.3%
- Buddhist 6%
- Sikh 0.4%
- Jewish 0.3%
- Shinto 0.1%

Christianity

Christianity is based on the teachings of Jesus Christ, who was born in Palestine. Christians believe that Jesus is the son of God and that he rose from the dead after being crucified on a cross. The Bible includes Jewish and Christian teachings.

Islam

Islam was founded in Arabia by the prophet Muhammad in about AD622. The Muslims' (followers of Islam) most sacred book is the Koran, which is the direct word of the one God, Allah. Islamic life is based on a set of rules called the five pillars of Islam.

Hinduism

Hinduism is the major religion of India. It began in about 1500BC. Hindus worship many gods. The three most important are Shiva, Vishnu, and Brahma. They believe in rebirth of the soul after death (reincarnation) and are born into social castes.

Buddhism

Buddhism is based on the teachings of an Indian prince, Gautama Siddharta, born in 563BC. He became known as Buddha, or Enlightened One. Buddhists believe in reincarnation and nirvana (peace). They meditate to achieve understanding.

Confucianism

Confucianism has no gods or belief in life after death, but stresses good conduct. It follows the teachings of Confucius, who was born in China about 551BC. Taoism, another Chinese religion, began about 300BC. Its many gods are taken from folk religions.

Judaism

Judaism was the first religion to teach that there is one God. Its main laws come from the Torah, the first five books of the Hebrew Bible. The ancient religion of the Jews was founded by Abraham, a Hebrew who lived in Canaan around 2000BC.

Sikhism

Sikhism was founded in India in the late 1400s by Guru (teacher) Nanak. The Sikhs believe in only one God. Sikh men wear five "k" symbols. They are kesh (uncut hair), kangha (comb), kara (bracelet), kaccha (breeches), and finally kirpan (dagger).

Shintoism

Shintoists worship the spirits of animals, rocks, trees, springs, and other elements of nature. Shinto is Japan's oldest religion. Until the mid-1900s the Japanese also worshipped their emperor, believing he was descended from the powerful Sun goddess.

NORTH AMERICA

North America is shaped like a giant triangle. The far north extends well above the Arctic Circle and is a frozen, treeless land. The continent's highest point, Denali (Mount McKinley), lies to the north in Alaska. The extreme south has both dry deserts and lush rain forests, with tropical vegetation covering many of the Caribbean islands. In between lie the forests of Canada and the northern United States of America. To the east the five Great Lakes form part of the continent's water drainage system. Vast prairielands of wheat spread right across the center of North America.

Constant movement of the Earth's crust causes earthquakes from time to time. California's Death Valley, the lowest point in North America, lies in an earthquake zone. This movement of the crust has also shaped the Rocky Mountains and the other great ranges that run down the western side of the continent, and is still shaping them today.

North America includes countries with all kinds of cultures, languages, and economies. These very different countries all have one thing in common—they were all controlled by a European power at one time. The countries of the North American mainland are now independent, but European links continue on some islands. The continent's largest island, Greenland, is a self-governing province of Denmark.

Bald eagle

The bald eagle is the national symbol of the U.S.A. It is found only in North America, and is a protected species.

■ CONTINENTAL FACTS

Area: 9,321,316 sq. mi. (including North and Central America, the Caribbean, and Greenland)
Population: 449,000,000 people
Independent countries: 23
Largest country: Canada
Smallest country: St. Kitts and Nevis
Highest point: Mount McKinley (Denali), Alaska, 20,322 ft.
Lowest point: Death Valley, California, 292 ft. below sea level
Largest lake: Lake Superior, Canada/U.S.A., 32,009 sq. mi.
Longest rivers: Mississippi-Missouri-Red Rock, 3,863 mi. Mackenzie-Peace,Canada, 2,635 mi.

Totem pole

Characters from Native American folklore are represented on traditional carved wooden totem poles in Canada.

Food and culture

Tortillas have been a basic Mexican food since before the time of the Aztec civilization. They are thin pancakes of corn or wheat flour. Tortillas can be eaten plain or stuffed with salad.

Canada

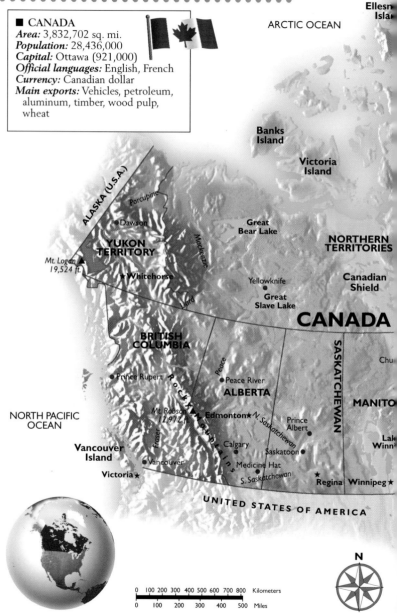

■ **CANADA**
Area: 3,832,702 sq. mi.
Population: 28,436,000
Capital: Ottawa (921,000)
Official languages: English, French
Currency: Canadian dollar
Main exports: Vehicles, petroleum,
aluminum, timber, wood pulp,
wheat

ARCTIC OCEAN

Ellesn
Isla

Banks
Island

Victoria
Island

Great
Bear Lake

NORTHERN
TERRITORIES

Canadian
Shield

ALASKA (U.S.A.)

Porcupine

Dawson

YUKON
TERRITORY

Mackenzie

Mt. Logan ▲
19,524 ft.

★Whitehorse

Yellowknife

Great
Slave Lake

Liard

CANADA

BRITISH
COLUMBIA

SASKATCHEWAN

Chu

Prince Rupert

Rocky

Peace

Peace River

ALBERTA

MANITO

NORTH PACIFIC
OCEAN

Mt. Robson ▲
12,972 ft.

Edmonton★

Fraser

Mountains

N. Saskatchewan

Prince
Albert

Calgary

Saskatoon

Lak
Winn

Vancouver
Island

Vancouver

Medicine Hat

Victoria ★

S. Saskatchewan

★
Regina

Winnipeg ★

UNITED STATES OF AMERICA

N

0 100 200 300 400 500 600 700 800 Kilometers

0   100   200   300   400   500 Miles

24

Inuit child

• • • • • • • • • • •

The Inuit people, descendants of some of Canada's original inhabitants, live in the frozen north. Today Inuit children wear modern clothes instead of traditional animal skins.

Canada's northern lands reach deep into the frozen Arctic, but most of the population lives in the south, close to the border with the United States. The country consists of ten provinces and two territories. It is full of contrasts, from fishing villages scattered along the Atlantic coast to major centers such as the French-speaking city of Montreal. The central plains form an immense grain-growing area, while rain-washed forests border the Pacific Ocean.

Canada was once a farming nation. Agriculture is still important, but now the country is highly industrialized and produces all kinds of manufactured goods.

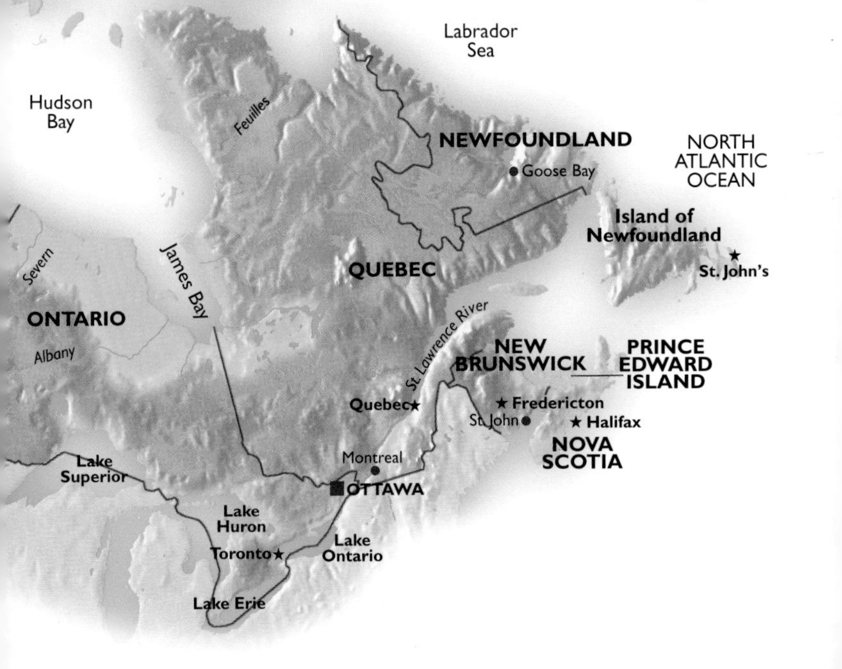

Baffin Bay

Baffin Island

Davis Strait

Labrador Sea

Hudson Bay

Feuilles

NEWFOUNDLAND

NORTH ATLANTIC OCEAN

• Goose Bay

Island of Newfoundland

Severn

James Bay

QUEBEC

★ St. John's

ONTARIO

Albany

St. Lawrence River

NEW BRUNSWICK

PRINCE EDWARD ISLAND

Quebec ★

★ Fredericton

St John ●

★ Halifax

NOVA SCOTIA

Montreal ●

Lake Superior

■ OTTAWA

Lake Huron

Toronto ★

Lake Ontario

Lake Erie

People and history

The Inuit people (Eskimos) were among the earliest inhabitants of Canada. Their word for community, *kanata*, gave Canada its name. The country itself has become a collection of communities. In the 1400s and 1500s the French and British came. They claimed lands in the east, attracted by rich fishing grounds and the chance to trade in furs. After bitter struggles during the 1700s, Britain took most of the French land and created two colonies, one English-speaking, the other French-speaking. These colonies were united as one nation in 1867.

Toward the future

Today almost half of all Canadians have British ancestors, while the other half are of French descent. The eastern province of Quebec is the center of French culture—over 75 percent of its population are French Canadians. In recent decades many French Canadians have campaigned for Quebec to become a separate nation. In 1992 the Inuit people, who live in the north, were granted a self-governing homeland called Nunavut, which will come into being in 1999.

Economy

Canada is a prosperous country. Most of its wealth comes from developing what occurs naturally —trees, fish, oil, natural gas, minerals, and water. It is the world's largest exporter of timber, paper, and other forest products. As well as being rich in all kinds of fish, Canada's huge lakes and rivers are dammed to provide electricity. Canada has a highly modernized manufacturing industry, producing everything from cars to canned fruit. However, most of the work force is employed in service industries such as education and finance.

Eastern Canada
• • • • • • • • • • • • • • •

A Nova Scotian boy learns to play the bagpipes. Nova Scotia means "New Scotland" and many of its people preserve the old Scottish ways.

Baffin Island
• •

Baffin Island in the Canadian Arctic is the home of Inuit people. They live in modern well insulated buildings but still use traditional kayaks or canoes.

Western Canada

The spectacular Athabasca Glacier is part of Jasper National Park, high up in the snow-capped Rocky Mountains in Alberta. It attracts many visitors from all over Canada and abroad.

Geography

Canada has more lakes and inland waters than any other country in the world. Forests cover almost half the country's total land area. The Coast Mountains and the snow-capped Rocky Mountains dominate western Canada. Beyond the Rockies the landscape softens into the Great Plains, with evergreen forests in the north and prairies in the south. Bordering the plains is a gigantic plateau called the Canadian Shield, which is made up of some of the oldest rocks in the world. To the far north, Canada extends to the frozen wastes of the Arctic Circle.

CN Tower

At 1,814 feet tall, the CN Tower is the world's tallest self-supporting structure. It stands on the waterfront in Toronto, overlooking Lake Ontario.

The space industry

The Canadarm is a robotic arm used on space shuttles. It is lifting an astronaut out of the shuttle to work on a satellite. Canada has a thriving space industry.

United States
of America

N

CANADA

Seattle

Olympia★ **WASHINGTON**

Portland Columbia

Salem ★

Cascade Range

OREGON

★ Boise **IDAHO**

Snake

Helena ★

Missouri

MONTANA

NORTH DAKOT

★ Bis

SOUTH DAKOT

WYOMING

N. Platte

Cheyenne ★

NEBRAS

Great Basin

Salt Lake City ★

Carson City ★

Sacramento ★

San Francisco

San Jose

Coast Ranges

UTAH

NEVADA

COLORADO

Colorado

S. Platte

★ Denver

Arkansas

KANS

Las Vegas ★

Grand Canyon

OKLAHOM

CALIFORNIA

Los Angeles ●

San Diego ●

Colorado

ARIZONA

★ Phoenix

Gila

Santa Fe ★

NEW MEXICO

Rio Grande

Pecos

● El Paso

TEXA

M E X I C O

San An

Rio Gran

| 0 | 100 | 200 | 300 | 400 | 500 | 600 Kilometers |
| 0 | | 100 | | 200 | | 300 Miles |

Statue of Liberty

This famous statue was a gift from France in 1886. It towers over New York Harbor, representing freedom for the American people.

■ UNITED STATES
Area: 3,602,816 sq. mi.
Population: 260,529,000
Capital: Washington, D.C.
(607,000)
Official language: English
Currency: U.S. dollar
Main exports: Aircraft, vehicles,
chemicals, coal, machinery, corn,
oil, soybeans, wheat

MAINE

VERMONT

NESOTA

Lake Superior

★ Augusta

NEW
HAMPSHIRE

MASSACHUSETTS

Montpelier ★

WISCONSIN

Lake
Huron

Lake
Ontario

MICHIGAN

Concord ★

neapolis

Lake
Michigan

NEW
YORK

Albany ★

★ Boston
RHODE IS.
★ Providence

St Paul

Madison

Lansing

Detroit

Lake Erie

Buffalo

Hartford ★

CONNECTICUT

★

Milwaukee

Chicago

Toledo

OHIO

PENNSYLVANIA

New York City

Des Moines

Harrisburg

NEW JERSEY

★Trenton

IOWA

INDIANA

Columbus

Pittsburgh

Philadelphia

ILLINOIS

Cleveland

Indianapolis

Cincinnati

WEST
VIRGINIA

Baltimore

★ Dover

DELAWARE

oln

Springfield

Ohio

Annapolis

WASHINGTON D.C.

Kansas
City

Jefferson
City ★

St. Louis

Frankfort ★

Charleston ★

Richmond ★

VIRGINIA

MARYLAND

eka

MISSOURI

KENTUCKY

NORTH
CAROLINA

Winston-Salem

★ Nashville

★ Raleigh

ARKANSAS

TENNESSEE

Memphis

Tennessee

SOUTH
CAROLINA

oma
ty

Arkansas ★

★ Columbia

River

Little Rock

MISSISSIPPI

Alabama

Atlanta
★

NORTH ATLANTIC
OCEAN

allas

LOUISIANA

Mississippi

Montgomery
★

GEORGIA

Jackson

ALABAMA

n

Baton Rouge ★

Tallahassee ★

Jacksonville

New Orleans

Houston

FLORIDA

Gulf of Mexico

Miami ●

The space shuttle
● ●

The U.S.A. pioneered the reusable space
shuttle. It is launched on the back of a
huge fuel tank powered by booster rockets.

29

The United States of America (U.S.A.) stretches a third of the way around the Earth, crossing eight time zones. The country is divided into 50 states. Two of these are isolated from the rest—Alaska, on Canada's western edge, and Hawaii, an island chain in the North Pacific Ocean.

The United States is ruled according to its famous Constitution, a document setting out how the country is governed. It allows individual states within the union to make some of their own laws. This helps each state to keep its individual character.

No other country in the world contains so much variety within its borders, from the icy lands of Alaska and the scorched deserts of the southwest, to the wide plains in the Midwest, the spectacular rock formations of Arizona and the subtropical forests of the southeast.

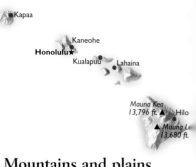

Mountains and plains

The United States has two great mountain chains, the forested Appalachian Mountains in the east and the snow-capped Rocky Mountains in the west. Massive plains stretch across the country between them. The northern and central parts of the plain are known as the Midwest. Much of this area is fertile farmland, with rich soil watered by major rivers such as the Mississippi, Missouri, and Ohio. These rivers are part of a water drainage system that includes the five Great Lakes in the northeast.

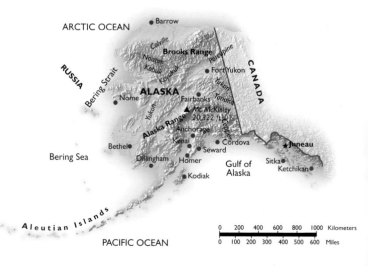

Citrus fruits
● ● ● ● ● ● ● ● ● ● ● ● ●

The U.S.A. is the world's leading grower of citrus fruits. Florida produces two thirds of the sweet oranges and grapefruit grown in the U.S.A.

Climate

Almost a third of Alaska lies north of the Arctic Circle, and some of this land is permanently frozen. The Midwest experiences floods and fierce tornadoes. All the southern states have hot summers and mild, or even warm, winters. In the southeast the climate is humid, with storms along the coast. However, there is little rainfall in the southwest, where deserts cover much of the land. In Hawaii, far out in the Pacific Ocean, the tropical climate hardly changes all year.

The White House
● ●

The White House in the city of Washington, D.C. is the official residence of the President of the United States.

The frozen north
● ●

The people of Alaska traditionally cross the ice and snow in sleds drawn by packs of husky dogs. The modern form of transport is the snowmobile, a motorized vehicle that runs on caterpillar tracks and skis.

Wheatfields near Correll
● ● ● ● ● ● ● ● ● ● ● ●

Rolling prairielands of wheat stretch as far as the eye can see all around the small town of Correll, near Des Moines in Iowa. Wheat is grown on a massive scale in America's fertile Midwest. During the harvest, combines travel in line for many days.

Birth of the U.S.A.

The first inhabitants of the U.S.A. were the American Indians. They lived here for 40,000 years before Europeans arrived in the 1500s.

By the 1700s British settlers had established 13 colonies on the east coast, which were ruled from Britain. When the colonies objected to British rule, the American Revolutionary War (1775-1783) broke out with Britain. The colonies won this war and became known as states. The United States was born. In 1787 the law of the land was drawn up. It was called the Constitution and still applies today.

The land of the free

From 1861–1865 a Civil War raged between the southern and northern states. The south wanted individual states to have more power and the right to use African slaves. The north won the war and slavery was finally abolished. Since then people from all over the world have settled in the United States. Steady population growth has helped to make it a very powerful country.

Chicago
∙ ∙

Two bascule bridges, operated by weights, rise to let ships pass on the Chicago River. In the center of the picture behind the first bridge is the Wrigley Building, Chicago's most famous landmark.

Jambalaya
∙ ∙ ∙ ∙ ∙ ∙ ∙ ∙ ∙ ∙ ∙ ∙ ∙

Jambalaya is a spicy rice and shrimp dish from New Orleans in the Deep South. It blends French and African cooking.

Monument Valley
∙ ∙ ∙ ∙ ∙ ∙ ∙ ∙ ∙ ∙ ∙ ∙ ∙ ∙ ∙ ∙ ∙ ∙

Millions of years of wind and rain have carved the dramatic rock shapes of Monument Valley in the southwest of the United States.

Leading the world

The United States has enormous economic power and leads the world in the production of manufactured goods. Its products include aircraft, electronic goods, cars, and chemicals. However, industries that produce services rather than goods are now the largest part of the U.S. economy. These include property, finance, insurance, entertainment, and healthcare.

The country's economy is largely based on a free market system. Companies are encouraged to compete against each other to win trade. Shares in companies are bought and sold at the New York Stock Exchange on Wall Street.

The enormous size of the United States has always been a great advantage. The land yields large amounts of natural resources such as petroleum, natural gas, coal and metal ores as well as fresh water. Vast forests meet most of the country's timber needs and many of its large rivers have been dammed to produce hydroelectric power.

Agriculture

Agriculture earns much less income than manufacturing and service industries, but is still carried out on a grand scale. The large farms of the Midwestern plains have made the United States the world's leading food producer. It is almost self-sufficient, unlike other countries that have to import food to feed their population. Kansas has earned the name "breadbasket of America" because it produces so much wheat. Other products include beef, dairy foods, soybeans, cotton, and tobacco.

Central America and

The landscape of Central America varies dramatically from sandy desert to tropical rain forest, and along the coast are humid mangrove swamps as well as palm-fringed beaches. The mountain ranges have many active volcanoes and there is a constant threat of earthquakes.

Great empires once flourished in these lands. From AD250 to 850 the Mayans built fabulous cities and temples here, where they worshiped

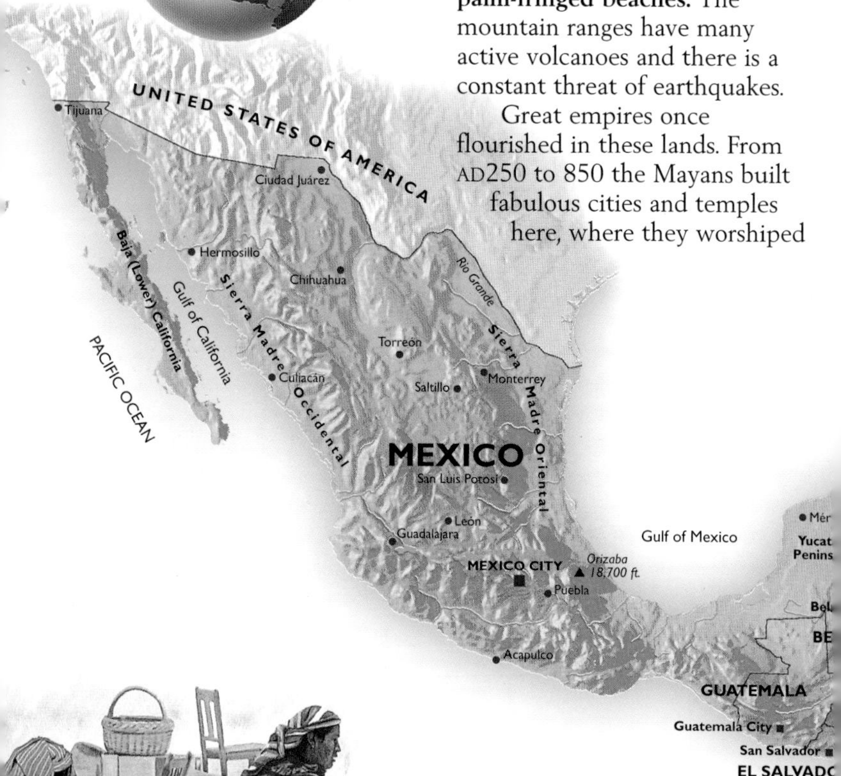

Tijuana

UNITED STATES OF AMERICA

Ciudad Juárez

Hermosillo

Chihuahua

Baja (Lower) California

Gulf of California

Sierra Madre Occidental

Rio Grande

Sierra Madre Oriental

Torreón

Culiacán

Saltillo

Monterrey

PACIFIC OCEAN

MEXICO

San Luis Potosí

León

Guadalajara

Gulf of Mexico

Mér

Yucat Penins

MEXICO CITY ■

Orizaba
▲ *18,700 ft.*

Puebla

Bel

BE

Acapulco

GUATEMALA

Guatemala City ■

San Salvador ■
EL SALVADO

Mexican market
. . . .
Stallholders prepare for a market in Oaxaca. Mexican farmers were among the first in the world to grow corn, tomatoes, avocados, and peppers.

the Caribbean

the Sun and the Moon. In the 1400s the powerful Aztec civilization stretched from coast to coast. Then in 1519 Spanish conquerors came, killing the Aztec rulers and plundering their gold. Central America remained under Spanish control for about 300 years before independence. Most people in Central America are *mestizos*, a mixture of Spanish and Native American, and Spanish is still spoken, along with English and Native American languages.

Havana cigars
. . . .

A worker hand-rolls a Havana cigar, Cuba's most famous export. The best cigar tobacco comes from plantations in the northwest.

N

BAHAMAS
Nassau ■

TURKS AND
CAICOS
ISLANDS (U.K.)

ATLANTIC OCEAN

ANTIGUA AND
BARBUDA

Straits of Florida

Havana ■

CUBA
● Camaguey

DOMINICAN
REPUBLIC

San Juan

HAITI
Port-au-Prince ■   ■ Santo
Domingo

PUERTO
RICO (U.S.A.)

ST. KITTS
AND NEVIS
DOMINICA

GUADELOUPE
(Fr.)

MARTINIQUE
(Fr.)

JAMAICA
Kingston

ST. LUCIA
ST. VINCENT

BARBADOS

CAYMAN
ISLANDS (U.K.)

GRENADA

CARIBBEAN SEA

NETHERLANDS
ANTILLES

TRINIDAD AND
TOBAGO

DURAS

igalpa

CARAGUA

anagua

Panama
Canal Panama City

■ San José

COSTA
RICA   PANAMA

COLOMBIA

**Black howler
monkey**
. . . .

The black howler monkey is found in Belize. It is at risk because the loss of forests is threatening its habitat.

0 100 200 300 400 500 600 700 800 Kilometers
0   100   200   300   400   500 Miles

35

Antigua and
Barbuda

Bahamas

Cuba

Dominican
Republic

Dominica

■ **MEXICO**
Area: 756,184 sq. mi.
Population: 91,261,000
Capital: Mexico City
(15,048,000)
Official language:
Spanish
Currency: Mexican peso
Main exports: Petroleum
and petroleum products,
vehicles, engines, cotton,
machinery, coffee, fish,
fertilizers, minerals

■ **PANAMA**
Area: 29,630 sq. mi.
Population: 2,515,000
Capital: Panama City
(585,000)
Official language:
Spanish
Currency: Balboa
Main exports: Bananas,
shrimp, coffee, sugar,
textiles, petroleum
products

■ **TRINIDAD AND
TOBAGO**
Area: 1,972 sq. mi.
Population: 1,260,000
Capital: Port-of-Spain
(59,000)
Official language: English
Currency: Trinidad and
Tobago dollar
Main exports: Petroleum
and petroleum products,
chemicals, rum, sugar

■ **BELIZE**
Area: 8,826 sq. mi.
Population: 205,000
Capital: Belmopan
(5,300)
Official language: English
Currency: Belize dollar
Main exports: Timber,
sugar, fish products,
clothes, fruit

■ **GUATEMALA**
Area: 41,857 sq. mi.
Population: 10,029,000
Capital: Guatemala City
(2,000,000)
Official language:
Spanish
Currency: Quetzal
Main exports: Coffee,
sugar, bananas, cotton,
beef, cardamom

■ **NICARAGUA**
Area: 50,233 sq. mi.
Population: 4,265,000
Capital: Managua
(683,000)
Official language:
Spanish
Currency: Córdoba
Main exports: Coffee,
cotton, sugar,
chemical products,
meat, bananas

■ **ST. LUCIA**
Area: 238 sq. mi.
Population: 139,000
Capital: Castries (54,000)
Official language:
English
Currency: East Caribbean
dollar
Main exports: Bananas,
coconuts, cocoa

■ **BAHAMAS**
Area: 5,328 sq. mi.
Population: 269,000
Capital: Nassau
(136,000)
Official language: English
Currency: Bahamian
dollar
Main exports: Mineral
fuels, chemicals, cement,
crayfish, rum

■ **HAITI**
Area: 10,667 sq. mi.
Population: 6,903,000
Capital: Port-au-Prince
(1,402,000)
Official languages:
French, Creole
Currency: Gourde
Main exports: Assembled
goods, coffee, sugar, sisal

■ **HONDURAS**
Area: 43,087 sq. mi.
Population: 5,595,000
Capital: Tegucigalpa
(679,000)
Official language:
Spanish
Currency: Lempira
Main exports: Coffee,
bananas, timber,
meat, sugar, shrimps,
lobsters

■ **JAMAICA**
Area: 4,394 sq. mi.
Population: 2,495,000
Capital: Kingston
(588,000)
Official language: English
Currency: Jamaican dollar
Main exports: Sugar,
bauxite, alumina,
bananas, fruit

St. Lucia   Haiti   Jamaica   Belize   El Salvador   Honduras

Barbados

Grenada

St. Kitts-Nevis

St. Vincent and Grenadines

Trinidad and Tobago

■ CUBA
Area: 42,615 sq. mi.
Population: 10,905,000
Capital: Havana (2,015,000)
Official language: Spanish
Currency: Cuban peso
Main exports: Sugar, minerals, fruit, fish, coffee

■ DOMINICA
Area: 288 sq. mi.
Population: 72,000
Capital: Roseau (9,000)
Official language: English
Currency: East Caribbean dollar
Main exports: Bananas, coconuts, fruit juices, essential oils

■ GRENADA
Area: 133 sq. mi.
Population: 92,000
Capital: St George's (36,000)
Official language: English
Currency: East Caribbean dollar
Main exports: Nutmeg, cocoa, bananas

■ PUERTO RICO
Area: 3,421 sq. mi.
Population: 3,620,000
Capital: San Juan (438,000)
Official language: Spanish
Currency: US dollar
Main exports: Sugar, coffee, chemicals, electronic equipment

■ BARBADOS
Area: 165 sq. mi.
Population: 260,000
Capital: Bridgetown (7,000)
Official language: English
Currency: Barbados dollar
Main exports: Sugar, chemicals, clothes, electronic equipment

■ DOMINICAN REPUBLIC
Area: 18,620 sq. mi.
Population: 7,608,000
Capital: Santo Domingo (1,314,000)
Official language: Spanish
Currency: Peso
Main exports: Sugar, molasses, ferronickel, gold, cocoa, coffee

■ ST. KITTS-NEVIS
Area: 100 sq. mi.
Population: 42,000
Capital: Basseterre (15,000)
Official language: English
Currency: East Caribbean dollar
Main exports: Sugar, cotton, electronics

■ ST. VINCENT AND THE GRENADINES
Area: 150 sq. mi.
Population: 111,000
Capital: Kingstown (27,000)
Official language: English
Currency: East Caribbean dollar
Main export: Bananas

■ ANTIGUA AND BARBUDA
Area: 169 sq. mi.
Population: 67,000
Capital: St. John's (30,000)
Official language: English
Currency: East Caribbean dollar
Main exports: Cotton, sugar, fruit, clothes, manufactured goods

■ COSTA RICA
Area: 19,643 sq. mi.
Population: 3,199,000
Capital: San José (297,000)
Official language: Spanish
Currency: Costa Rican colón
Main exports: Coffee, textiles, bananas, sugar, cocoa

■ EL SALVADOR
Area: 8,088 sq. mi.
Population: 5,517,000
Capital: San Salvador (1,523,000)
Official language: Spanish
Currency: El Salvador colón
Main exports: Coffee, sugarcane, shrimps, flowers, textiles, corn, cotton

Nicaragua   **Mexico**   **Panama**   **Puerto Rico**   **Guatemala**   **Costa Rica**

Mexico

The powerful Aztec civilization flourished in Mexico from the mid-1400s with its capital at Tenochtitlán (now Mexico City). In 1519 Spanish conquerors started a bloody war in the Gulf of Mexico. They defeated the Aztecs, and Spain ruled for the next 300 years. Mexico became independent in 1821, but war with the United States followed and Mexico lost much of its land. This troubled period ended in 1917 and a new system of laws was adopted. Now most Mexicans live in large cities where influences from the United States and Europe are transforming everyday life. However, many people in the villages still speak one of the Native American languages as well as Spanish and the whole country keeps alive festivals that are 5,000 years old.

Fishing in Mexico

These fishermen on Mexico's Lake Patzcuaro are using butterfly nets. They make their boats look as if they had wings.

Coffee

Coffee is an important crop in Central America and the Caribbean. It thrives in the cool foothills of the mountains.

Ripe berries

Roasted beans

Coffee plant

Mexican dancers

At Veracruz dancers called voledores (fliers) perform acrobatics on top of a swinging pole. They are taking part in a traditional festival.

Nicaragua

Nicaragua gained independence from Spain in 1821. Civil war then divided the country for nearly a century. In 1912 US troops became involved and stayed for 20 years. The military leader, Anastasio Somoza, gained control in 1936. His family ruled as dictators until 1979, when left-wing rebels called Sandinistas took over. Groups known as the contras (which means against) disagreed with the Sandinistas over how the country should be run and fought them, supported by the United States.

The Sandinistas were defeated in the 1990 elections and the war ended. Today most Nicaraguans work on small farms or large plantations. Rich landowners established the plantations, but the government now owns many of them.

The Caribbean

The West Indies is a chain of islands that stretches around the Caribbean Sea. It is made up of the Bahamas, the Lesser Antilles, and the Greater Antilles (Cuba, Hispaniola, and Puerto Rico). Hispaniola is divided into two countries, Haiti and the Dominican Republic.

The Caribbean islands are rocky, fringed with coral reefs and covered with tropical forests. Most islanders are descendants of slaves who were brought from Africa to work on plantations growing bananas, sugarcane, and spices. The rest are of European, Indian, Chinese, or mixed descent.

Tobago
. . . .

Tobago's white beaches attract many tourists. The warm Caribbean Sea is ideal for sailing, swimming, and snorkeling.

The Panama Canal
. . . .

This important shipping route links the Atlantic and Pacific. It has made Panama City an international finance center.

Economy

The tropical climate is ideal for growing sugarcane, tobacco, fruit, cotton, and coffee. These nations used to depend on farming and fishing for their income. However, since the discovery of oil in the Gulf of Mexico, more people are leaving the countryside to work in mining and other industries. Often they have to live in shanty towns because the cities are not growing fast enough to house them. Another important industry is tourism. Visitors come to enjoy the Caribbean beaches and relaxed way of life.

SOUTH AMERICA

South America has landscapes of immense variety. The hot dusty grasslands of the southern Pampas are cattle-ranching country. In the west, coffee grows in the cool valleys of the high Andes Mountains. The Atacama Desert is one of the driest places in the world. The basin of the mighty Amazon River is covered with dense rain forest, one of the last great wildernesses on Earth.

The diverse Indian cultures developed brilliant civilizations. The last of them were destroyed in the 1500s by conquerors from Spain. As European settlers flooded to the continent, many Indian tribes were wiped out by disease. In the 1820s the settlers began to break away from their European rulers in bloody wars of independence.

Many of the new nations prospered, but usually the settlers grew rich while the Indians stayed poor. Poverty led to strikes and riots and in most countries the military seized power. Over recent decades more democratic governments have been elected. There have been efforts to preserve political stability and improve living standards. The continent has a wealth of natural resources, but earning money from them often upsets the delicate balance of nature.

Kamayura

The Kamayura are just one of the many native peoples living in the rain forests. The men wear earrings and brightly colored feather headdresses.

Gauchos

A gaucho—a skilled Argentine cowboy—wields his lasso. Gauchos wear high boots with spurs, felt hats, and baggy trousers.

■ SOUTH AMERICA FACTS
Area: 6,765,440 sq. mi.
Population: 316,000,000
Independent countries: 12
Highest point: Mt. Aconcagua
(22,835 ft.)
Longest rivers: Amazon (3,998 mi.),
Rio de la Plata-Parana (2,480 mi.)
Highest waterfall: Angel Falls (3,212 ft.)
Largest lake: Maracaibo
(5,194 sq. mi.)

The Iguaçu Falls

• • • • • • • • • • • • • • • • •

The Iguaçu Falls is a string of 275
spectacular waterfalls on the border
between Argentina and Brazil. The
water cascades down drops
of up to 230 feet.

Scarlet macaw

• • • • • • • • • • • • • • • •

The scarlet macaw is the brightest
of the parrot family. Macaws live
in the high canopies of rain forest
trees and crack nuts with their
powerful beaks.

The Andean States

Colombia, Ecuador, Peru, and Bolivia are dominated by the towering peaks of the Andes. Many of these mountains are active volcanoes that occasionally erupt. Moving plates deep under the earth also pose the threat of earthquakes.

The Andes was the homeland of the Incas, who ruled a rich and civilized empire here until the Spanish conquest 500 years ago. Descendants of the Incas still farm the ancient terraced fields on steep mountain ridges, growing potatoes and tomatoes, the original crops of South America. The mountains are also mined for their rich deposits of emeralds, gold, and tin, and in Colombia some farmers hide secret crops of the illegal and highly profitable drug cocaine.

Dense tropical rain forest spreads east of the Andes to the heart of the continent. Valuable deposits of oil have been found here, endangering the future of the forest, its animals and Native American inhabitants.

Cathedral in Ecuador

This Roman Catholic cathedral is in Cuenca, a city founded by Spanish conquerors in 1557. Christianity is the official religion in the Andean states.

Way of life

Most people of the Andean states live in modern cities. They work in mines that yield emeralds or coal, or in factories that produce a wide range of goods, from steel to cement or clothing. The high-rise buildings in downtown areas are often surrounded by large suburbs of shanty towns where the poorer people live. Some people lead a more traditional life as farmers in mountain villages. They often supplement their income by producing crafts to sell to tourists. Only a few groups,

Boat people

The Uru people, living on Lake Titicaca in Peru, travel in boats made of reeds. They also use reeds to make their houses, which are built on rafts of reeds floating on the lake.

Map scale:
0 250 500 750 1000 1250 Kilometers
0 100 200 300 400 500 600 700 Miles

PANAMA

Barranquilla

Andes Mts.

Medellín

VENEZUELA

Bogotá

Meta

Cali

COLOMBIA

Orinoco

N

Quito

ECUADOR

Guayaquil

Amazon

Iquitos

BRAZIL

Chiclayo

Trujillo

Huascarán
22,205 ft.

PERU

Lima

Cuzco

Guaporé

BOLIVIA

El Misti
19,100 ft.

Lake
Titicaca

La Paz

Santa Cruz

Arequipa

Lake
Poopó

Sucre

CHILE

PARAGUAY

ARGENTINA

Bolivian women
• • • • • • • • • • • •

*In La Paz, Bolivia,
women traders gather to
sell corncobs. They wear
colorful traditional
clothes, including these
highly distinctive hats.*

such as the Waorami, still live in
the depths of the rain forest. They
hunt monkeys, sloths, and tapirs
with poison-tipped arrows.
They clear land to build
villages of thatched huts,
grow small amounts of crops,
then move on after harvest
to hunt and fish. Many
Native Americans speak
their own languages,
such as Quechua, but
Spanish is the
official language of
the Andean States.

Emeralds
• • • • • • • • • • • • • • • •

*Colombia produces about half
the world's emeralds. These
brilliant green gemstones are
often set in Colombian gold to
make valuable jewelry.*

Peruvian musician
• • • • • • • • • • • •

*A Native American
musician, wearing
a traditional hat
and cape, plays
a haunting
tune on the
panpipes.*

43

Farming and fishing

On the steamy coastal plains west of the Andes, the climate is ideal for growing cotton, bananas, cocoa, and sugarcane. Abundant rain falls in the mountains, and it is cooler there. A wide range of crops, including coffee, is grown on the fertile hillsides. There are cattle farms on the lush rolling grasslands and northern plains. Fishing is another major source of income. The Pacific yields large catches of herring and tuna.

Inca civilization

The original inhabitants of the Andean States were Native American peoples. The most brilliant of these were the Incas, who came to power in the 1400s. They followed the Huari and the Chimu peoples in a series of civilizations that first developed in Peru about 3,000 years ago. The Inca period was famous for its monumental architecture and for beautifully crafted gold and pottery. The Incas used precious metals freely because they were readily available. Careful organization and a good network of roads enabled them to hold together a vast empire that covered all the central Andes.

Spanish conquest

In 1532 the conqueror Francisco Pizarro arrived from Spain in search of treasure, and set about killing the Incas and destroying their empire. During the 300 years that Spain ruled the Andean states, thousands of Spanish

La Paz, Bolivia
. . . .
Skyscrapers tower against a backdrop of mountains in Bolivia's financial and administrative capital, La Paz. The country's legal capital is Sucre.

Bolivian trader
. . . .
This man is selling traditional shawls and blankets. Native Americans make these woolens for their own use as well as to sell to tourists.

Oil workers in Ecuador
. . . .
Workers drill for oil in the remote eastern rain forests on the border with Peru. Both Ecuador and Peru lay claim to this region, intending to exploit its valuable resources.

settlers arrived. They brought slaves from Africa to work alongside Native American survivors on sugarcane plantations. Many groups of Native Americans were destroyed or killed by disease. Only a few of the original communities still lead traditional lifestyles today.

Independence

In the early 1800s the Andean States won their independence from Spain in a series of bloody battles. But independence did not win peace, and political unrest is never far from the surface in these countries today. A deep cultural and economic division still exists between the Native Americans and the descendants of the Spanish settlers.

Peruvian dagger

Dating back some 700 years to the Chimu period, this ornate dagger is shaped like a man. It is made of gold and studded with the semiprecious stone turquoise.

El Dorado

This gold model shows El Dorado (The Golden Man) on his raft. Legendary tales of this rich king drew Spanish conquerors in search of gold.

■ **COLOMBIA**
Area: 438,889 sq. mi.
Population: 33,951,000
Capital: Bogotá (4,922,000)
Official language: Spanish
Currency: Colombian peso
Main exports: Coffee, emeralds, petroleum, coal, flowers, meat

■ **ECUADOR**
Area: 109,000 sq. mi. (Galapagos Islands 3,015 sq. mi.)
Population: 10,981,000
Capital: Quito (1,101,000)
Official language: Spanish
Currency: Sucre
Main exports: Bananas, petroleum, shrimp, coffee, cocoa, sugar

■ **PERU**
Area: 478,301 sq. mi.
Population: 22,454,000
Capital: Lima (5,760,000)
Official languages: Spanish, Quechua
Currency: New sol
Main exports: Copper, lead, fish products, iron, zinc, oil, coffee, llama and alpaca wool, cotton, sugar

■ **BOLIVIA**
Area: 422,294 sq. mi.
Population: 7,065,000
Capitals: Sucre (106,000), La Paz (670,000)
Official language: Spanish
Currency: Boliviano
Main exports: Natural gas, oil, tin, zinc, silver, gold, coffee, sugar

Colombia

Ecuador

Peru

Bolivia

Brazil and its neighbors

0 250 500 750 1000 1250 Kilometers
0 250 500 750 Miles

Caribbean Sea

TRINIDAD AND TOBAGO

Caracas

Maracaibo

COLOMBIA

VENEZUELA

Orinoco

Georgetown

Paramaribo

GUYANA

SURINAME

Cayenne

FRENCH GUIANA

Guiana Highlands

Orinoco

Branco

Negro

Japurá

Manaus

Amazon

Macapá

Belém

ATLANTIC OCEAN

Amazon

PERU

Juruá

Purus

Madeira

Tapajós

Xingu

Araguaia

Tocantins

Fortal

Guaporé

BOLIVIA

BRAZIL

Brazilian Highlands

Parnaíba

São Francisco

Re

Salvad

Mato Grosso Plateau

BRASÍLIA

Goiânia

Belo Horizonte

PARAGUAY

Paraná

Rio de Janeiro

São Paulo

Iguaçu Falls

Curitiba

ARGENTINA

Uruguay

URUGUAY

Pôrto Alegre

N

Simón Bolívar

This statue in Caracas, Venezuela, commemorates Simón Bolívar. He led the revolution against Spanish rule in the early 1800s.

Brazil is full of natural wonders. The brown sluggish waters of the mighty Amazon River snake their way through the world's largest area of dense rain forest. The forest spreads into Guyana, Suriname, and French Guiana and is known only to the Native Americans who hunt and fish there, their lives barely touched by the modern world.

Brazil also has rich mineral resources and fertile soils that produce coffee, cocoa, and sugarcane. Every year Brazilians celebrate the most famous carnival in the world, which has its center at Rio de Janeiro. This city shows the huge gap between rich and poor in Brazil, with modern high-rise buildings surrounded by slums.

The country has serious economic problems. Huge areas of the Amazon rain forest are being destroyed to make new farmland and grazing land, which means that rare animals and medicinal plants are lost forever. This has become an environmental issue of worldwide concern.

Space station, French Guiana

• •

An Ariane rocket stands in the Assembly Hall of the European Space Agency station at Kourou. Rockets launched from this station on the coast of French Guiana often carry satellites into space.

Brazil nuts

• •

Many Brazil nut trees in the Amazon rain forest are being cut down to make farmland that will yield less nutritious crops from the same amount of land.

Piranha fish

• • • • • • • • • • •

Meat-eating piranha fish have very sharp teeth. If a wounded animal falls into the Amazon River they strip its flesh in minutes.

Chilies

• • • • • • • • • • • •

Red and green chili peppers are dried and ground to make cayenne pepper. This fiery spice is named for the capital of French Guiana, Cayenne.

47

Carnival
● ● ● ● ● ● ● ● ● ●

*Carnival-goers
celebrate in Brazil.
Carnival is a five-
day party that
marks the start of
Lent, 40 days
before Easter.*

History

During the 1500s Europeans
invaded South America, drawn by
the lure of gold. They killed many
Native Americans and forced
others into slavery. Brazil was
ruled by the Portuguese,
Venezuela by the Spanish, Guyana
by the British, and Suriname by
the Dutch. Independence came to
most of the continent in the
1800s, but French Guiana is
still a dependency of France
and receives aid from the
French government.

Suriname horse dance
● ● ● ● ● ● ● ● ● ● ● ● ● ● ● ● ●

*Descendants of the Javanese
people who came to live in
Suriname keep their heritage alive
by performing a traditional dance.*

Industry and agriculture

Brazil is South America's leading
industrial nation and the world's
largest producer of coffee and
sugarcane. There are enormous
reserves of iron ore here and the
country's mines also yield gold
and diamonds. Large deposits of
oil have been found in the
Amazon basin.

Venezuela is the richest
nation in South America, due to
valuable reserves of oil discovered
in Lake Maracaibo. Oil exports
earn about three quarters of
Venezuela's income. Industry is
centred in cities on the coastal
strip, where products range from
cars to medicines. Venezuela also
has valuable deposits of bauxite
and manganese and thriving new
aluminum and steel plants.

Forest products

Guyana is one of the world's
biggest producers of bauxite, and
also has deposits of manganese
and gold. Like its neighbor
Suriname, it grows sugarcane and
bananas. Cutting valuable timber
for export in the countries of
the Amazon Basin has driven
Native Americans deeper into
the rain forests.

Cathedral in Brasília

Imposing sculptures line the route to the spectacular modern cathedral in Brasília, the capital city of Brazil.

Rain forest wildlife

South America has one of the richest varieties of wildlife in the world. In the Amazon basin alone there are at least 44,000 different kinds of plants, 2,500 types of river fish, and 1,500 species of birds. In the rain forest there are large bird-eating spiders and mammals include armadillos, jaguars, and sloths. In the rivers are manatees, freshwater dolphins, giant catfish, and electric eels. Of the thousands of forest insects, many have yet to be identified and studied.

Hallacas

Hallacas is a Venezuelan Christmas turnover of meat in corn meal pastry. It is eaten with bread and ham (right).

■ **VENEZUELA**
Area: 350,592 sq. mi.
Population: 20,712,000
Capital: Caracas (1,045,000)
Official language: Spanish
Currency: Bolivar
Main exports: Coffee, oil, iron ore, textiles, fruit, aluminum

■ **GUYANA**
Area: 82,634 sq. mi.
Population: 816,000
Capital: Georgetown (188,000)
Official language: English
Currency: Guyana dollar
Main exports: Gold, aluminum, sugar, rice, rum, bauxite, timber

■ **SURINAME**
Area: 62,972 sq. mi.
Population: 446,000
Capital: Paramaribo (201,000)
Official language: Dutch
Currency: Surinam guilder
Main exports: Alumina, bauxite, aluminum, shrimp, rice, bananas, timber

■ **FRENCH GUIANA**
Area: 32,109 sq. mi.
Population: 108,000
Capital: Cayenne (42,000)
Official language: French
Currency: French franc
Main exports: Shrimp, prawns, rice, timber and metal products

■ **BRAZIL**
Area: 3,272,013 sq. mi.
Population: 159,143,000
Capital: Brasília (1,597,000)
Official language: Portuguese
Currency: Real
Main exports: Iron ore, coffee, fruit, timber, sugar, vehicles, beef

Guyana

Suriname

French Guiana

Brazil

The Southern States

Kilometers
0 25 50 75 100

Miles
0 10 20 30 40 50 60 70

PERU
BOLIVIA
Arica
Iquique
Atacama Desert
Antofagasta
CHILE
PARAGUAY
Gran Chaco
Asunción
BRAZIL
Tucumán
Salado
Paraná
Uruguay
ARGENTINA
Córdoba
Rosario
URUGUAY
Valparaíso
Santiago
Aconcagua 22,835 ft.
Montevideo
BUENOS AIRES
Concepción
Pampas
Colorado
Bahía Blanca
Mar del Plata
Negro
Andes
PATAGONIA
Chubut
N
FALKLAND ISLANDS (U.K.)
Tierra del Fuego
Cape Horn
SOUTH GEORGIA (U.K.)

Paraguayan lace

A Paraguayan lacemaker works at a bedspread in traditional Guaraní (Indian) style. Flowers, birds, animals, and decorative patterns are created out of the lace, which is called ñandutí, the Guaraní word for spiderweb.

Seat of government in Argentina

The Congress Building in Buenos Aires, Argentina's capital city, is built in the French style. Buenos Aires is often referred to as the "Paris of South America." Buenos Aires is the Spanish for "fair winds" and the city is a major international port.

Around 500 years ago only Indians lived in this region, including the Incas in northern Chile, the Guaraní in the tropical northeast, and the Guajira in the far south. Then in the 1500s the Spanish fortune hunters arrived and began to take control. Gradually the indigenous peoples fell victim to European diseases, died in slavery, or were massacred.

The wars of independence fought with Spain during the early 1800s did not lead to peace. They were followed instead by bitter internal strife, economic crises, and periods of military rule. In recent decades the Southern States have become democratically elected republics.

Most of the people of this region are of European or mixed descent. Native Americans form only a small minority. Immigrants continue to flood into prosperous Argentina. It is proud of being a multicultural land, with a population including British, Hungarians, Italians, and Lebanese. All keep alive their national customs and traditions.

Steam train
• • • • • • • • • • • • • • • • • • • •

This steam train is used to transport tropical hardwood across Paraguay. The timber is a valuable resource, but its harvest is wiping out large tracts of rain forest.

Montevideo, Uruguay
• • • • • • • • • • • • • • • • • •

A statue in Uruguay's capital celebrates the early Spanish settlers. They crossed the country with ox-drawn carts to build towns and farms inland.

Spectacular landscapes

Chile is the longest, thinnest country in the world. The fertile central area is occupied by wheatfields and orchards. To the north lies the arid Atacama Desert. The far south is a land of forests, mountains, and glaciers. Oil and natural gas have been found among the southern islands, and the country is also rich in minerals. Most Chileans live in the coastal cities and work in industry. Chile and Argentina are divided by the majestic Andes Mountains.

51

Beef country

The Spanish gave Argentina its name. They believed they would find rich deposits of silver here and called the land after *argentum*, the Latin word for silver. As it turned out, they were proved wrong. Argentina's greatest treasure is its lush pastureland and fertile soil, which stretches across into Uruguay and eastern Paraguay.

Argentina's economy was founded on the meat and leather industry in the 1800s. Its best grazing land is the Pampas, rolling plains where cowboys called *gauchos* herd prime beef cattle. Much of the Pampas is divided into huge *estancias* (ranches) owned by a wealthy few.

In the warm foothills of the Andes is a rich farming area, producing wheat, oranges, and grapes. The west of Paraguay and Argentina's far northwest are known as the Gran Chaco, an area of bleak salt marshes. To the south lies Patagonia, a scrubby land that bakes in summer and freezes in winter. Most people here are sheep farmers.

Maté teadrinker
● ●

This man sips maté tea from a gourd, through a metal tube. Maté is a hot bitter tea drunk all over South America.

■ **CHILE**
Area: 283,264 sq. mi.
Population: 13,813,000
Capital: Santiago (4,859,000)
Official language: Spanish
Currency: Chilean peso
Main exports: Copper, iron, fruit, wood pulp

■ **PARAGUAY**
Area: 156,355 sq. mi.
Population: 4,643,000
Capital: Asunción (945,000)
Official language: Spanish
Currency: Guaraní
Main exports: Cotton, soybeans, timber, meat, vegetable oil

■ **URUGUAY**
Area: 67,735 sq. mi.
Population: 3,149,000
Capital: Montevideo (1,384,000)
Official language: Spanish
Currency: Uruguayan peso
Main exports: Meat, leather, hides, wool, fish, textiles

■ **ARGENTINA**
Area: 1,103,263 sq. mi.
Population: 33,778,000
Capital: Buenos Aires (9,928,000)
Official language: Spanish
Currency: Peso
Main exports: Wheat, corn, meat, hides, wool, tannin, linseed oil

Chile

Paraguay

Uruguay

Argentina

Valuable tourist trade

The majority of Uruguayans live along the south coast, which overlooks the wide estuary of the Río de la Plata (Plate River) and the Atlantic Ocean. In summer large numbers of tourists flock to the sandy beaches of this long coastline. Just inland begin fertile, low-lying plains, where crops such as rice, tangerines, peaches, and grapes grow through the hot summers and mild winters, watered by regular rainfall.

Beyond the plains lie rich pastures with huge farms that raise cattle and sheep. Leather, wool, and meat products are a vital source of income to Uruguay. A great deal of meat is eaten in the country and beef is Uruguay's favorite meal.

Parliament in Paraguay

The Paraguay National Congress Parliament Building stands in the nation's capital, Asunción. The city was founded in the 1500s by Spanish conquerors on their way to seek gold in Peru.

Fertile farmlands

Landlocked Paraguay is a hot and humid country, divided in two by the Paraguay River. To the east are lush grasslands and thick forests. Almost all Paraguayans live here, mainly ranching cattle and farming sugarcane, rice, coffee, and soybeans. To the west the Gran Chaco is a vast plain of salt marshes, thorny scrub, and sparse grass. Paraguay remains a poor country, but its fertile farmlands and potential for hydroelectric power promise a brighter future.

Chilean copper mine

Chuquicamata in northern Chile is one of the largest open-cast copper mines in the world. Copper is Chile's main export.

A ruined church in Argentina

These ruins at San Ignacio are a legacy of the Jesuits, who came to the region in the 1600s to convert the Guarani peoples.

EUROPE

London's Buckingham Palace

Buckingham Palace, at the heart of Britain's capital, London, is the official residence of the royal family. Today European kings and queens have limited powers.

Throughout its history Europe has greatly influenced world politics. The ancient Greeks invented democracy in about 450B.C. This system, where the government is chosen by the people, is widespread today. By the 1700s Europeans were practicing colonialism. Powerful seafaring nations such as Spain, the Netherlands, and Britain ruled much of the world. They grew rich from exploiting Asia, Africa, and the Americas. Many of these colonies did not gain their independence until this century.

Both World Wars began in Europe. After World War II (1939–1945) the continent split into communist countries in the east, led by the Soviet Union, and noncommunist countries in the west, supported by the United States. Europe became the center of a power struggle, known as the Cold War, between the two sides. The Cold War ended with the collapse of communism in the 1980s and 1990s, but conflict between ethnic groups and economic problems caused new tensions in eastern Europe. By 1996, 15 western European nations had joined the European Union. This organization works to unite the different countries of Europe politically and economically.

■ CONTINENTAL FACTS

Area: 4,051,190 sq. mi. (including the European parts of Russia and Turkey)
Population: 584,000,000 (excluding Russia)
Independent countries: 44 (excluding Russia and Turkey)
Largest country: Russia (about 25% of Russia is in Europe; 75% in Asia)
Smallest country: Vatican City
Highest point: Mt. Elbrus, Russia (18,481 ft.)
Largest lake: Caspian Sea (143,250 sq. mi., partly in Europe, partly in Asia)
Longest river: Volga (2,290 mi.)

Spanish oranges

Spain, in sunny southern Europe, is one of the world's largest exporters of citrus fruits. Bitter oranges from Seville are made into marmalade.

European Union
. . . .

The flags of the European Union fly outside the Council of Europe in Strasbourg, France. The European Union was set up in the 1950s. It has grown since then and today has 15 member nations. Its object is to unify European politics and economics.

Hedgehog
. . . .

The hedgehog is a nocturnal animal that rolls up into a ball when attacked. Its fur has evolved into spines that keep enemies at bay. Hedgehogs hibernate in their nests over winter.

Scandinavia and

Finland

Isafjördur
Vatneyri • Hólmavík • Saudárkrókur • Húsavík
Bordeyri • Akureyri
Seydisfjördur •

ICELAND
Vatnajökull

Akranes
■ **REYKJAVIK**
Keflavík •
▲ *Oraefajökull 6,952 ft.*

Vestmannaeyjar

Scandinavia and Finland are among the northernmost inhabited areas of the world. Northern Scandinavia lies inside the Arctic Circle, and is called the Land of the Midnight Sun, because it is light for 24 hours a day around midsummer and dark for much of the day in December. While the north of this area has an Arctic climate, the south is kept mild by the Gulf Stream, a warm ocean current.

The rugged scenery of these northern countries is the legacy of the last Ice Age. The ice caps and glaciers are the remains of a huge sheet of ice that covered much of northern Europe 10,000 years ago. In Norway the glaciers gouged out steep valleys and sea inlets called fjords, deep enough to carry ocean-going ships. In Finland and Sweden the ice ground out thousands of lakes, and dotted the lakes and the coastline with tiny islands. The southernmost country of the group, Denmark, has a low-lying mainland and nearly 500 islands. Its territory includes two self-governing protectorates, the windswept Faeroes and the vast Arctic wastes of Greenland, which is on the other side of the Atlantic Ocean east of Canada.

The island of Iceland is known as the Land of Ice and Fire because it has active volcanoes and geysers set in a dramatic landscape of icefields and glaciers. As recently as 1963 a volcano under the sea created a new offshore island, Surtsey, as lava bubbled up from the ocean floor.

Åles

• B

• Sta

Fish processing
. . . .

Fish are sorted at a processing plant in Tromsø. The catch of herring, whiting, cod, and haddock is frozen and canned as well as dried in the traditional way.

N

ARCTIC OCEAN

Hammerfest • • Vadsø
• Kirkenes

• Tromsø

NORTH ATLANTIC
OCEAN

▲ Mount Haltia
4,344 ft.

L a p l a n d

Narvik •

Svolvær •   ▲ Kebnekaise
              6,926 ft.   • Kiruna   • Sodankylä

Bodø •

                                              • Rovaniemi

              • Övertorneå

                                   • Kemi

Mosjøen •   • Luleå

              Skellefte
         Storuman •   • Oulu

                 Ume   • Skellefteå

SWEDEN   • Umeå   • Kokkola   • Kuopio

Trondheim •   Joensuu •
                Östersund   • Vaasa

jansund •   • Kaskö   • Jyväskylä

                                       FINLAND
                        Sundsvall •
lhøpiggen
8,100 ft.   Tampere •
                 • Särna
                                                  • Lahti
mmer •
ORWAY   Vösterdal   Turku • **HELSINKI** ■
                        • Gävle   **Åland**
   OSLO ■   **Is.**   Gulf of Finland

         Karlstad •   **STOCKHOLM** ■   **ESTONIA**
en •   • Örebro • Uppsala
      Lake
      Vänern

ansand   Baltic Sea
rrak •   • Linköping
borg Göteborg • • Borås
              • Västervik
                        Gotland

              • Borgholm

ENMARK
nus •   • Karlskrona
  COPENHAGEN ■
• Odense • Malmö   Kristianstad

Gulf of Bothnia

Kattegat

RUSSIA

GERMANY

```
0        100      200      300   Kilometers
|--------|--------|--------|
0    50      100      150      200   Miles
```

■ **NORWAY**
Area: 148,747 sq. mi.
Population: 4,312,000
Capital: Oslo (460,000)
Official language: Norwegian
Currency: Norwegian krone
Main exports: Oil and oil products,
  natural gas, ships, fish, paper, wood
  pulp, machinery

■ **SWEDEN**
Area: 172,964 sq. mi.
Population: 8,716,000
Capital: Stockholm (685,000)
Official language: Swedish
Currency: Krona
Main exports: Vehicles, machinery,
  iron, steel, paper products

■ **FINLAND**
Area: 129,985 sq. mi.
Population: 5,067,000
Capital: Helsinki (502,000)
Official languages: Finnish, Swedish
Currency: Markka
Main exports: Timber, vehicles,
  paper products, machinery, ships,
  clothes, furniture

■ **DENMARK**
Area: 16,560 sq. mi.
Population: 5,189,000
Capital: Copenhagen (1,343,000)
Official language: Danish
Currency: Danish krone
Main exports: Meat, fish, dairy
  products, electrical equipment,
  machinery, transportation equipment

■ **ICELAND**
Area: 39,593 sq. mi.
Population: 263,000
Capital: Reykjavik (101,000)
Official language: Icelandic
Currency: Krona
Main exports: Fish and fish
  products, shellfish, crustaceans,
  animal feed, aluminum, iron,
  steel, diatomite

Sami people in Lapland
● ● ● ● ● ● ● ● ● ● ● ● ● ● ● ● ● ● ●

*Today only a small number of Sami
(Lapp) people live the traditional nomadic
way of life, keeping reindeer for their meat,
milk, and hides.*

The riches of the sea

In these northern countries, the sea plays an important role in people's lives. Fishing has long been one of the most important industries of Scandinavia, helped by the warm ocean currents that flow in the Atlantic and keep the coasts free of ice. Norwegians have exported dried fish since the early 1200s. Today fish is still dried, as well as frozen and canned. Fleets from Iceland, Norway, and Denmark trawl the North Atlantic and Greenland Sea in search of cod, herring, capelin, and haddock. Shipbuilding is another major industry. The shipyards of Finland specialize in icebreakers and ferries that cross the rough northern waters. Since oil was discovered in the North Sea in the early 1960s, the Norwegians have become expert at constructing oil rigs as well as building fishing vessels in their many natural harbors.

Swedish ski school

In Sweden children old enough to walk are ready to learn to ski. Skiing is a useful way of getting about and a popular sport.

Natural resources

The prosperity of these modern nations is built on the development of their natural resources. Oil and gas are drilled in the North Sea. The Danes have developed wind turbines to harness wind power and generate electricity. Rivers in Sweden and Finland are dammed to produce hydro-electric power. Dense forests provide plentiful timber for furniture and paper making. To ensure future supplies of timber and protect the environment, forests are continually replanted.

Volcanic rocks

Black rocks rise from the waters of Lake Myvatn in Iceland. They were formed from the cooled lava of ancient volcanoes.

The Scandinavian people

The people of Scandinavia share a common history. In the early Middle Ages they were Vikings, the seafarers and warriors who sailed to Iceland, Greenland, and North America. They also raided and settled in parts of Russia and northern Europe.

The earliest known people to settle in Scandinavia were the Sami (Lapps). Their descendants still live in Lapland, north of the Arctic Circle. Some Sami lead the traditional nomadic way of life, herding reindeer and fishing. Others work in factories or mines.

These five northern nations are peaceful and prosperous and enjoy some of the best standards of living in the world. People pay high taxes, but have many welfare benefits, including free healthcare, education, and pensions.

Danish pastries

These sweet rolls are rich, flaky, and often iced. The Danes eat them with coffee at any time of the day.

Netherlands, Belgium and Luxembourg

The Netherlands, Belgium, and Luxembourg form a region known as the Low Countries. By the 1300s the French dukes of Burgundy were in control of this area. In the early 1500s the Low Countries joined the immense empire of the Habsburg family, whose lands included Spain and Austria. The region grew rich through trade. Then many people in the Low Countries joined the Protestant religion introduced from neighboring Germany. They resented being ruled by Spain, a Roman Catholic country, and rebelled against the Habsburgs. After many battles they shook off Spanish power in 1648.

During the 1600s the Netherlands became one of the world's leading seafaring nations and acquired a large overseas empire.

Dutch cheese

Round, wax-covered cheeses are carried on sleds to market in Alkmaar, a popular destination for tourists. The Netherlands exports large amounts of cheese to countries all over the world.

Trade with the Dutch East Indies (Indonesia) brought great wealth to the Netherlands. At the end of the 1600s Dutch power began to decline. Belgium broke away to become a separate nation in 1830, followed by Luxembourg in 1867. In this century the three countries have rebuilt close links and prospered. In 1948 they forged an economic union known as Benelux. In 1957 they were founder members of the European Union.

Belgian carnival

Belgians dress up as giants for an annual parade around town streets. The costumes have peep-holes in their skirts so the people hidden inside can see where they are going.

Grape harvest

● ● ● ● ● ● ● ● ● ● ● ●

Harvesters tip grapes
into a vat to begin
making Moselle wine.
The grapes are grown
on Luxembourg's steep
terraced hillsides by the
Moselle River.

West Frisian Islands

Waddenzee

Leeuwarden

Groningen

IJsselmeer

AMSTERDAM ■

Enschede

Leiden

NETHERLANDS

● The Hague

Lek

Arnhem

● Rotterdam

Maas

Nijmegen

Breda

Tilburg

Eindhoven

GERMANY

N

● Ostend

Antwerp

Bruges

Ghent

Leie

Schelde

Maastricht

■ **BRUSSELS**

BELGIUM

Liège

● Mons

Namur

Meuse

Botrange ▲
2,277 ft.

● Charleroi

Sambre

Ardennes Mts.

F R A N C E

Bastogne

LUXEMBOURG

■ **LUXEMBOURG**

| 0 | 25 | 50 | 75 | 100 | Kilometers |
| 0 | 10 | 20 | 30 | 40 | 50 | 60 | Miles |

Economy

The standard of living in these countries is high. Belgium is one of the most heavily industrialized countries in Europe and steel manufacturing is its most important industry. Rich deposits of iron have made Luxembourg another leading steel producer. Its capital, Luxembourg City, is an international center of banking and finance.

The Netherlands is famous worldwide for its dairy produce, greenhouse vegetables, cut flowers, bulbs, and seeds. Dutch factories produce a wide range of goods from electrical appliances to textiles and chemicals.

■ **BELGIUM**
Area: 11,736 sq. mi.
Population: 10,010,000
Capital: Brussels (951,000)
Official languages: Dutch, French
Currency: Belgian franc
Main exports: Iron, steel, machinery, transportation equipment, plastics, chemicals, processed food, cut diamonds, textiles

■ **NETHERLANDS**
Area: 15,964 sq. mi.
Population: 15,287,000
Capital: Amsterdam (1,092,000)
Official language: Dutch
Currency: Guilder
Main exports: Dairy produce, flower bulbs, vegetables, petrochemicals, electronic equipment

■ **LUXEMBOURG**
Area: 996 sq. mi.
Population: 380,000
Capital: Luxembourg City (76,000)
Official languages: French, German, Letzebuergesch
Currency: Luxembourg franc
Main exports: Iron, steel, textiles, machinery, chemicals, plastics

---

Geography

The word Netherlands means lowlands. The country is almost entirely flat and much of the land lies below sea level. There are large areas of polder, land that has been drained or reclaimed from the sea. The delta region of the southwest is protected against flooding by a series of huge dams and floodgates.

Flat farmland reclaimed from the sea also forms much of Belgium's coastal lowlands. These rise to fertile plateaus in the centre of the country and to the wooded hills of the Ardennes in the southeast. The Ardennes extend into the north of Luxembourg and the Sauer and Moselle Rivers form its eastern boundary. The south, with its green pastures and fertile farmland, is known as the Bon Pays (Good Land).

Dutch windmills

• •

The Netherlands is famous for tulips and windmills. Wind power was used to drain the land. Today this work is done by modern pumps.

The member countries of the European Union fly their flags in a brisk wind outside the Secretariat of the European Parliament in the capital of Luxembourg. Luxembourg City is a major center of finance and administration.

A carpet of flowers

A carpet of begonias decorates a square in the center of Brussels, Belgium's capital. This display is created every other August.

Copper butterfly

The copper butterfly lives in Belgium's central lowlands. Numbers are decreasing because of the draining of its marshland habitat.

People

The people who live in the Netherlands are known as the Dutch, and their country is sometimes called Holland. They and their lowland neighbors are mainly descended from Germanic peoples called the Franks, Frisians, and Saxons, who settled in this region about 2,000 years ago.

The Belgians are divided into two main ethnic groups. The Dutch-speaking Flemings live in northern Belgium and the French-speaking Walloons in the south. To reduce tensions between the two, Belgium has created separate regions that have considerable control over local matters. The people of Luxembourg speak French, German, and Letzebuergesch. Most people of this region live in cities and work in industry.

Transportation

The flat landscape of the Netherlands is cut by a network of rivers, canals, and dikes. Barges make their way up and down the waterways. In Belgium, the Meuse and Schelde rivers have been important trade routes for centuries. Goods are also carried across the heavily industrialized lowlands by truck and train. Spreading suburbs and high-rise apartment buildings are found in most cities, but the downtown areas have often changed little for centuries. There are fine old brick houses that date back to the 1600s. The flat ground makes bicycles the ideal form of personal transportation.

The British Isles

The British Isles consists of England, Scotland, and Wales on the mainland, and the island of Ireland. Northern Ireland belongs with England, Scotland, and Wales to the United Kingdom (U.K.), while the south is the independent Republic of Ireland.

The U.K. was the first nation in the world to change from an agricultural economy to an industrial one. It has a large population for its size. But outside its crowded towns and cities there is beautiful countryside—the heather-covered glens of Scotland, the deep valleys and mountains of Wales, and the rolling fields of England and Ireland. A mild, wet climate makes much of the land green and fertile.

During the Middle Ages the countries of the British Isles were often at war with one another. From the 1500s, they began to make peace. They joined forces to conquer territories overseas and build up a vast empire. In 1921 southern Ireland left the Union to become a republic. Britain's political power declined in the 1900s, although it played a leading role in the two World Wars. By the 1960s the British Empire had broken up and most of Britain's colonies had become independent. In 1973 it joined the European Union.

Lloyds Building

The headquarters of Lloyds Bank was completed in 1986. It stands in the City of London, the financial center of the U.K.

Stonehenge

Some of the stones used to build the prehistoric temple at Stonehenge were dragged from a site 250 miles away. It must have taken many years to build.

Carrauntoohill
3,414 ft

N

Orkney Is. • Kirkwall

• Thurso

• Stornoway

Outer
Hebrides

North West Highlands

Skye

Loch
Ness

• Inverness

• Peterhead

Lerwick

Shetland Is.

North Sea

Mallaig

SCOTLAND

▲ Ben Nevis
4,406 ft.

• Aberdeen

Grampian
Highlands

Tay

• Oban

Perth •

• Dundee

ATLANTIC
OCEAN

Glasgow

■ Edinburgh

Clyde

• Ayr

Southern Uplands

Tweed

Londonderry

NORTHERN
IRELAND ■ Belfast

• Stranraer

Newcastle •

Tyne

Carlisle

• Durham

• Middlesbrough

• Sligo

• Armagh

Lake
District

Pennines

Swale

IRELAND

• Dundalk

Isle of
Man

Irish Sea

Blackpool •

Leeds •

• Kingston-upon-Hull

way

• Athlone

Shannon

Liffey

■ DUBLIN

Bradford •

Manchester •

Liverpool •

• Sheffield

erick

• Carlow

ENGLAND

Wrexham •

Derby •

• Nottingham

• Tipperary

Cambrian
Mts

Wolverhampton •

Trent

• Norwich

• Waterford

Aberystwyth •

Birmingham •

• Coventry

Peterborough •

Cambridge •

Severn

Northampton •

• Ipswich

WALES

Wye

Carmarthen •

• Luton

• Colchester

Swansea •

Gloucester •

Oxford •

LONDON ■

• Canterbury

Cardiff ■

• Bristol

Reading •

Thames

• Dover

ATLANTIC OCEAN

Exmoor

Salisbury •

Southampton •

• Portsmouth

• Folkestone

• Brighton

Dartmoor

• Exeter

Bournemouth •

Land's
End

• Plymouth

• Penzance

English Channel

0   50   100   150   200 Kilometers
0   50   100 Miles

CHANNEL
ISLANDS

Industry

The U.K. is a major industrial nation. During the 1800s industries such as textiles, steel-making, shipbuilding, and engineering were developed. They were fueled by coal, the U.K.'s biggest natural resource at that time. Recently, newer industries such as electronics, food processing, and chemicals have grown in importance. Most people now work in services such as education, healthcare and tourism. Today the U.K.'s most important natural resources are the large fields of oil and natural gas that lie beneath the North Sea.

In the Republic of Ireland, three out of five people live in towns or cities. Many have jobs in service industries or the manufacture of textiles and glass.

Irish fishermen

● ●

Two Irish fishermen pull a lobster pot back into shape before going to sea once again. Shellfish accounts for nearly a third of the Republic of Ireland's earnings from fishing. Ireland also has many lakes (loughs) and rivers teeming with trout and salmon.

■ **UNITED KINGDOM**
Population: 57,826,000
Currency: Pound sterling
Main exports: Manufactured goods

■ **ENGLAND**
Area: 50,133 sq. mi.
Capital: London (6,680,000)
Official language: English

■ **WALES**
Area: 7,984 sq. mi.
Capital: Cardiff (279,000)
Official languages: Welsh, English

■ **SCOTLAND**
Area: 29,664 sq. mi.
Capital: Edinburgh (438,000)
Official language: English

■ **NORTHERN IRELAND**
Area: 5,428 sq. mi.
Capital: Belfast (284,000)
Official language: English

■ **REPUBLIC OF IRELAND**
Area: 27,016 sq. mi.
Population: 3,563,000
Capital: Dublin (916,000)
Official languages: Irish, English
Currency: Punt
Main exports: Livestock, dairy products, whiskey, machinery, chemicals, manufactured goods

United Kingdom

Northern Ireland

England

Wales

Scotland

Republic of Ireland

Farming

In the U.K. only about two percent of the population is employed in farming. However, much of the country is intensively farmed to produce grain, fruit, and vegetables. Dairy cattle graze on the green pastures of western England and sheep feed on the uplands of Scotland and Wales. Much of the U.K.'s ancient forest and woodland has been destroyed over the years, but large conifer plantations provide timber for building and paper making.

Farming is vital to the economy of the Republic of Ireland. Its exports include butter, cheese, and other dairy products, natural fibers, whiskey, and beer.

Giant's Causeway
●●●●●●●●●●●●●●●●●●●●●●

The Giant's Causeway is a spectacular rock formation that forms part of the rugged coast of County Antrim in Northern Ireland.

Firth of Forth Bridge
●●●●●●●●●●●●●●

The Forth Bridge, opened in 1890, has two arches either side of Inchgarvie Island. About 60,000 tons of steel were used to build the bridge.

Cliffs of Dover
●●●●●●●●●●●●●●●●●●●●●●●●●●

The white cliffs of Dover on the English Channel symbolize home to English people returning by sea from the Continent.

Conflict in N. Ireland

Northern Ireland suffers from a political and religious divide. From 1969 a war raged there between the Irish Republican Army (IRA), Catholics who want the whole of Ireland to be an independent republic, and Protestant Loyalists, who want to maintain ties with Britain. A fragile peace declared in 1994 was followed by further violence.

67

Germany

Germany lies at the heart of Europe. Surrounded by nine other countries, its natural boundaries are two stretches of coastline in the north, the Rhine River in the southwest, and the Bavarian Alps in the southeast. It is a fertile land with wide rivers and thick forests. Tourists visit all year round to enjoy beautiful scenery and fine architecture. Germany has rich natural resources, which have helped it rise above the devastation of the two World Wars to become one of the world's leading industrial nations. Its major cities are international centers of trade and banking.

Very few Germans work on the land. Most live in towns and cities, where the country's thriving industries are based. Since the 1950s many people from Turkey, Italy, and Yugoslavia have also come to the country to work. Although this is a modern nation of city-dwellers, old customs have not been forgotten. Some Germans still wear national dress

Fairs and festivals

A giant mask adds color to the annual Museum Embankment festival held in Frankfurt. Carnivals are enjoyed throughout Germany.

for special occasions. Medieval traditions are preserved by townspeople who regularly perform plays that were written centuries ago.

Political protest has been common in western Germany since the 1960s. Today Germans often gather to protest modern issues. These include pollution, nuclear power, and the rise in racism that has recently occurred in Germany and other parts of Europe.

Ulm Cathedral

Ulm Cathedral was founded in 1377, but not completed until 1890. Its steeple is the tallest in the world, rising more than 500 ft. above the city on the Danube River.

68

N

DENMARK

NORTH SEA

BALTIC SEA

Flensburg

Kiel

Neumünster

Stralsund

Rostock

Lübeck

Schwerin

Wilhelmshaven

Bremerhaven

Hamburg

Bremen

Lüneburg

Elbe

Weser

Celle

Aller

Hannover

Brunswick

Brandenburg

■ BERLIN

Frankfurt an der Oder

POLAND

Oder

Bielefeld

Weser

Leine

Hildesheim

Harz Mts.

Magdeburg

Elster

Münster

Paderborn

Dessau

Cottbus

Neisse

Ems

Rhine

Essen

Dortmund

Kassel

Halle

Leipzig

Duisburg

Wuppertal

Mühlhausen

Elbe

Düsseldorf

Dresden

Cologne

Marburg

Erfurt

Chemnitz

Aachen

Bonn

Geissen

Gera

Zwickau

Ore Mountains

Koblenz

Plauen

Eifel

Moselle

Rhine

Wiesbaden

Frankfurt-am-Main

GERMANY

Main

CZECH REPUBLIC

Trier

Mainz

Darmstadt

Bayreuth

URG

Mannheim

Würzburg

Bamberg

Saarbrücken

Heidelberg

Nuremberg

Bohemian Forest

Karlsruhe

Heilbronn

Regensburg

Stuttgart

Danube

Ingolstadt

Passau

Swabian Jura

Augsburg

Ulm

Black Forest

Munich

Freiburg

AUSTRIA

Lake Constance

ALPS

▲ Zugspitze 9,721 ft.

SWITZERLAND

FRANCE

NETHERLANDS

| 0 | 50 | 100 | 150 | Kilometers |

| 0 | 25 | 50 | 75 | 100 | Miles |

Geography

Germany's low sandy coast looks out on to the stormy North Sea and Baltic Sea. The two seas are linked by the Kiel Canal, a busy shipping channel. Inland is a wide flat plain of heathland and timber plantations. Crops are grown in the broad river valleys. In the valley of the Ruhr River, rich deposits of coal and metal ores are mined.

In the center is a rugged landscape of plateaus, forested mountains, gorges, and rushing rivers. Vineyards and pasture where sheep graze cover the western hills, while wheat and barley grow in the fertile valleys. In the southwest lies the Black Forest, named for its dark fir trees. In the far southeast are the soaring Bavarian Alps. The highest point in Germany, the Zugspitze, is in this region.

Frankfurt stock exchange

Dealers are busy trading on the floor of the Frankfurt stock exchange. Frankfurt, on the Main River, is a major center of industry and finance. The city often hosts international trade fairs.

History

People have lived here since ancient times. For most of its history this has been a divided land made up of many small states. Germany's defeat in World War I (1914-1918) left the country in crisis. The Nazis (National Socialists) came to power, promising to make Germany great again. Led by Adolf Hitler, the Nazis aimed to create a master race and killed millions of Jews, Poles, Russians, and political opponents. Germany was defeated again in World War II (1939-1945) and separated into two parts—the Federal Republic of Germany in the west and the German Democratic Republic in the east. In 1990 the two parts were reunited amid great celebrations on both sides.

Wurst

Wurst means sausage and Germany is said to have over 1,500 different kinds! Wurst in rolls is often sold as a snack on the street.

■ **GERMANY**
Area: 137,127 sq. mi.
Population: 81,187,000
Capital: Berlin (3,438,000)
Official language: German
Currency: Deutsche Mark
Main exports: Machinery, iron, steel, transportation equipment, textiles, chemicals, minerals, wine, lignite

Economy

Germany is Europe's leading industrial nation. It is Europe's largest auto manufacturer and a world leader in the production of chemicals for medicines, plastics, and paints. In western Germany most farms are small and many are only operated part-time. In eastern Germany large farms that were run by the state are now being broken up and sold to individuals.

After World War II Germany's cities and factories were devastated and the country was divided. West Germany was helped by the United States, Britain, and France to rebuild its economy. In 1957 it became a founder member of the European Union. East Germany was under communist rule and had state-run industries. It spent a lot of money on creating jobs and on social welfare, but had very few consumer goods. After reunification in 1990 the east joined the west's economic system, which caused high prices and unemployment in the east. These problems can be solved by

The Bavarian Alps
. . . .

Berchtesgaden is a ski resort set high up in the Bavarian Alps. Many mountaineers go there to climb Mount Watzmann.

Cologne Cathedral
. . . .

The twin spires of the cathedral dominate Cologne's skyline. Building began in the 1200s but was not completed until 1880.

Switzerland, Austria, and Liechtenstein

Switzerland is a land of towering snowy mountains, high waterfalls and long misty lakes. The Alps form a series of high ranges in the south and east, while the rainy conifer forests of the Jura Mountains line the western border with France. Below these peaks alpine pastures provide summer grazing for cattle and goats. Very little Swiss land is suitable for growing crops, except for hay and livestock fodder. Rushing rivers are dammed for hydroelectric power, but Switzerland has few other natural resources. Raw materials are imported and skilled craftspeople turn them into precision goods such as watches, clocks, and electrical equipment.

About three quarters of Austria lies in the snow-capped, thickly forested Alps. Deer and small numbers of chamois live in these mountains. Austria has broad green valleys, rushing rivers, and deep lakes. Cattle graze the high pastures while barley, rye,

Hallstatt, Austria

This small market town rises steeply from the shore of Lake Halstatt. Because its cemetery suffers from lack of space, older bones are removed and stored on show in a charnel house in the mountainside.

and potatoes are grown in the Vienna Basin, the flat valley of the mighty river Danube. Much of the land is too rugged for agriculture, but by using modern farming methods Austria is able to produce three quarters of the food its people need. Grapes are grown for wine. Timber for wood pulp and paper is cut from forests that are replanted according to strict conservation laws. Austria is a highly industrialized country, though most of its population now works in service industries such as retail, banking, tourism, and healthcare.

Swiss fondue

Fondue is a dish of Swiss cheese heated in a pot with white wine. Bread is dipped into the cheese speared on forks. Fondue means melted in French.

Vienna's Burgtheater

Vienna's imposing Burgtheater was built in the late 1800s. At this time the capital of Austria was one of the most important cultural centers in the world. It was particularly known for its rich musical life.

White-tailed eagle

The survival of the white-tailed eagle is now endangered. These majestic birds have been hunted close to extinction. Some may still be seen circling over the Austrian Alps in winter.

Liechtenstein

Liechtenstein was formed in 1719 when Prince Johann-Adam Liechtenstein joined together the two territories of Vaduz and Schellenberg, formerly parts of the Holy Roman Empire. His descendants still rule here, though laws are now passed by an elected parliament. Women in Liechtenstein did not gain the right to vote until 1984.

Vaduz Castle, Liechtenstein

Vaduz Castle is the home of the Prince of Liechtenstein. It overlooks a steep hillside high above the country's capital. The castle's fortifications date from the 1500s.

■ SWITZERLAND

Area: 15,810 sq. mi.
Population: 6,938,000
Capital: Bern (299,000)
Official languages: German, French, Italian, Romansch
Currency: Swiss franc
Main exports: Machinery, chemicals, clocks and watches, precision instruments, textiles, clothes, foods including chocolate

■ AUSTRIA

Area: 32,236 sq. mi.
Population: 7,988,000
Capital: Vienna (1,540,000)
Official language: German
Currency: Schilling
Main exports: Machinery, iron, steel, transportation equipment, timber, paper and paper pulp, textiles

■ LIECHTENSTEIN

Area: 625 sq. mi.
Population: 28,000
Capital: Vaduz (5,000)
Official language: German
Currency: Swiss franc
Main exports: Machinery, chemical products, textiles, pottery, dental products, stamps

Austria—history

The early inhabitants of Austria mined and traded in iron and salt. Celtic peoples moved here around 400BC, then in 15BC Austria was conquered by the Romans. From the 1200s a powerful family called the Habsburgs ruled Austria, making it the center of a vast empire that grew to include Spain, Hungary and the Netherlands. Austria began to lose power in the 1800s and by 1918 the Habsburg empire was finished. The country was torn apart during the two World Wars, but since the 1950s Austria has built up its economy and become politically stable. It joined the the European Union in 1995.

Tirol, Austria

• •

Hikers admire the view near Vent in the Tirol, the mountainous west of Austria. Hiking and skiing are two favorite pastimes for the Austrian people.

Viennese festival

Imaginatively dressed professional clowns perform stunts and mime in the streets of Vienna during Vienna festival week.

The Matterhorn, Switzerland

Chamois leap gracefully across the rocks beneath the east face of the Matterhorn, which stands on the Swiss–Italian border.

Switzerland—history

More than 2,000 years ago the Romans conquered the land that is now Switzerland, and called it the province of Helvetia. In 1291 the Swiss cantons, or provinces, began to fight to break away from the Holy Roman Empire. They gained independence in 1648.

Since 1815 the country has remained neutral, avoiding wars that have swept across Europe. Switzerland's neutrality has attracted many organizations that depend on international cooperation, such as the United Nations. Peace and stability have also helped the country prosper as a world center of banking.

Liechtenstein—economy

Liechtenstein's population is no bigger than that of a small town. This country has strong ties with neighboring Switzerland and uses Swiss currency. Dairy cattle graze the alpine pastures, while barley and fruit are grown in the valleys. However, only three percent of the population works in agriculture. Since the 1950s Liechtenstein has developed as an industrialized nation with one of the highest standards of living in the world. Banking and tourism are its main industries, and the production of textiles, chemicals, and pottery is also important. More revenue comes from the foreign businesses that have their headquarters here, attracted by Liechtenstein's low taxes.

France

France is a country of varied and beautiful landscapes, modern industries, historic towns, and great cities. It has produced great thinkers, politicians, writers, painters, musicians, architects, scientists, moviemakers, and fashion designers. It is also famous for its wines and food, which are often said to be the best in the world. Each of France's 22 regions has its own traditional customs, foods, and drinks, and several also have their own languages, although French is spoken everywhere.

The French Revolution of 1789 made France one of the first European nations to overthrow its king and set up a republic. The monarchy was restored for a time in the 1800s, but a republic was established once more in 1871. Since then, France has been a democratic republic almost continuously. The government is headed by a president, who appoints a prime minister. The capital, Paris, has long been the center of power. However, the regions of France now have a greater say in government.

Sacré Coeur

Sacré Coeur Cathedral at the heart of Paris has long been a destination for pilgrims.

Brest
Quimper
Lorie

The majority of French people live in towns and cities. They work in manufacturing or service industries, such as education and catering. Their standard of living is high and most workers enjoy long summer holidays. In rural areas the majority work in agriculture and the countryside is dotted with small family farms and vineyards that are passed from one generation to the next.

Breton lacemaker

This woman is working a traditional lace mat. She is from Brittany, in northwest France. Her traditional dress includes a tall headdress made of lace called a coiffe.

76

N

CORSICA
(France)

• Bastia

Ajaccio •

• Bonifacio

0   50   100   150   200 Kilometers
0   50   100 Miles

Dunkerque
Calais •   • Lille
Boulogne •
English Channel   • Arras   BELGIUM
Cherbourg •   • Dieppe   • Amiens   Charleville-Mézières   LUXEMBOURG
Le Havre •   • Rouen   Reims   Metz •   GERMANY
• Caen   Seine   PARIS ■   Marne   Châlons-sur-Marne   Nancy   Strasbourg •
-Malo   FRANCE   • Chartres   • Troyes   Vosges Mountains   Colmar •   Rhine
• Rennes   Fontainebleau   Seine   Moselle   Mulhouse •
• Le Mans   • Orléans   Saône   Besançon •   SWITZERLAND
aire   Loire   Cher   Bourges   Dijon •   Doubs   Jura Mountains
Angers •   • Tours   Loire
• Nantes   • Poitiers   Mâcon •   Saône
La Rochelle •   Montluçon •   Loire   • Lyon   Mt. Blanc 15,771 ft.
• Cognac   Limoges •   Clermont-Ferrand •   • St-Etienne   Isère   • Grenoble   ITALY
Mt. Dore 6,188 ft.   Central   Isère   Isère   Alps
of   Bordeaux •   Massif   Cère   • Valence   Drac
ay   Dordogne   Lot   Rhône   Durance   MONACO
Garonne   Lot   Aveyron   Avignon •   Verdon   Nice
Montauban •   Tarn   Nîmes •   Aix-en-Provence   Cannes
ritz   Adour   Toulouse •   Montpellier   Durance   • Marseille
• Bayonne   Garonne   Carcassonne •   • Béziers   Toulon
• Pau   Ariège   Aude   Mediterranean Sea
• Lourdes   Pyrenees   • Perpignan
SPAIN   ANDORRA

77

Economy

Rich farmland and a mild climate make France an important agricultural nation. Wheat, sugar beet, vegetables, and apples are grown in the north. Dairy cattle graze the lush pastures of the northwest, producing creamy butters and cheeses. Vines growing grapes for the wine industry flourish nearly all over the country. In the south and southwest there are fields of sunflowers and corn, as well as orchards of peaches, plums, and cherries. A large timber industry is based on the country's vast forests.

France's natural resources include bauxite (used to make aluminum), iron ore, coal, and oil. Mountain streams and rivers are harnessed to produce hydroelectric power and France has also built many nuclear power stations. French factories produce chemicals, textiles, and electronic equipment. About half the labor force works in service industries.

Monaco
● ●

The tiny principality of Monaco attracts visitors from all over the world who come to gamble in its famous casinos and gaming halls.

Pont du Gard
● ● ● ● ● ● ● ● ● ● ● ●

This Roman aqueduct was built to carry fresh water to the city of Nîmes in southern France. The Romans built many fine cities and roads during their occupation of France from about 50BC until the AD400s.

A varied landscape

The French climate is mild and rainy along the Atlantic coast, but farther inland, the summers are hot and the winters cold. The landscape is immensely varied. In the north are fertile plains crossed by broad meandering rivers. To the west, craggy headlands jut into the stormy Atlantic. In the east, forested hills rise to high snow-capped mountains, and in the south, sunny beaches line the glittering Mediterranean Sea. France's borders are marked by mountains. The Vosges and Jura ranges run along the German and Swiss frontiers, and the Pyrenees join France to Spain. The mighty Alps rise along the Italian border, with gleaming glaciers and walls of rock towering above mountain pastures where cattle graze.

Provence
• • • • • • • • • • • • • • • • • •

Fields of scented lavender color a hillside in Provence in the south of France. Lavender and other flowers including roses are used to make perfume at Grasse, the international center of the industry.

Quiche Lorraine
• • • • • • • • • •

This dish comes from Lorraine, in northeastern France. The crisp pastry shell is filled with beaten eggs, cream, cheese, seasoning, and chopped bacon.

Pyrenean desman
• • • • • • • • • • • • • • • • • •

The Pyrenean desman, a long-nosed water mole, lives in the fast-flowing streams of the Pyrenees. Pollution is threatening its survival.

79

Spain and Portugal

Spain and Portugal are cut off from the rest of Europe by the rocky Pyrenees, a range of snow-capped mountains. The two countries together form the Iberian Peninsula. Spain's interior is a plateau, a vast area of high flat ground that is hot and dusty in summer. High rainfall to the north makes the coast there green and fertile. In the south, a fierce sun beats down on vineyards and groves of olives and oranges. Because most of Spain has such little rain, farmers need to irrigate their crops by pumping water to them.

Many Spaniards are employed in industry, and Spain is one of the largest car manufacturers in Europe. Others work in catering and tourism, looking after the visitors who come to enjoy their country's warm climate and golden beaches.

Portugal lies to the west of Spain, on the Atlantic Ocean. The north of the country is rocky, with a mild, damp climate, while the south is flat, and very hot in summer. Much of the land is covered in forests of valuable cork oaks. Cork from these trees is exported all over the world, and so is port, one of the wines for which Portugal is famous.

80

N

Bay of Biscay

FRANCE

ANDORRA

Pyrenees

Andorra la Vella

San Sebastián

Bilbao

Vitoria

Pamplona

Figueras

Gerona

Burgos

Logroño

Ebro

Arga

Gallego

Cinca

Manresa

Tarrasa

Barcelona

Soria

Duero

Ebro

Jalón

Saragossa

Lérida

Reus

SPAIN

Caspe

Tarragona

Tajuña

Tajo

Tortosa

dalajara

Alcalá de Henares

Teruel

Morella

Vinaroz

Mijares

MENORCA

MALLORCA

Mahón

DRID

Aranjuez

Cuenca

Turia

Castellón de la Plana

Palma

Manacor

do

Villarroblédo

Júcar

Valencia

IBIZA

Ciudad Real

Albacete

Alcoy

Ibiza

rtollano

Segura

Alicante

Mediterranean Sea

Linares

Murcia

Jaén

Lorca

Cartagena

Aguilas

Granada

ierra

evada

Almería

Motril

The Parade of the Giants

•••••••••••••••••••••••••••••

The Parade of the Giants takes place every year
in Toledo, Spain. Children and grown-ups dress
up in masks as devils, animals, and clowns,
and sing and dance through the streets.

81

People

The people of the Iberian peninsula are very diverse. The Basque people of the north speak Euskara, a language not connected with any other in Europe. The Galicians of the far northwest trace their history back to the ancient Celts, and their traditions include bagpipe-playing. In the south, the influence of Moorish conquerors can still be seen in the architecture and farming methods, while Romany gypsies have left their mark on the passionate singing and dancing of flamenco. Everyone joins together to celebrate the many religious festivals, fairs, and fiestas. Most people enjoy watching bullfights. Because of the fierce heat, businesses close in the middle of the day and people take a siesta (nap) after lunch.

■ SPAIN
Area: 194,026 sq. mi.
Population: 39,143,000
Capital: Madrid (2,910,000)
Official language: Spanish
Currency: Peseta
Main exports: Vehicles, wine, machinery, fruit, vegetables, olive oil, chemicals, textiles, iron, steel

■ ANDORRA
Area: 173 sq. mi.
Population: 48,000
Capital: Andorra la Vella (19,000)
Official language: Catalan
Currency: French franc, Spanish peseta
Main exports: Clothes, mineral water, tobacco

■ PORTUGAL
Area: 35,299 sq. mi.
Population: 9,860,000
Capital: Lisbon (831,000)
Official language: Portuguese
Currency: Escudo
Main exports: Clothes, textiles, cork, port and other wines, machinery, transportation equipment, footwear, paper, timber products, canned fish

Portugal

Andorra

History

About 5,000 years ago the Iberians came to Spain and Portugal from North Africa. Later on, Greeks, Romans, and Moors from North Africa also settled. In the 1400s explorers from Spain and Portugal conquered much of South America. They also established colonies in Africa and Asia. From the 1600s their power declined as their colonies broke away. During the 1900s, Spain and Portugal were ruled by harsh dictators. In the 1970s they became democracies. Today both belong to the European Union.

The Monument to the Discoveries

• •

This sculpture in Portugal's capital Lisbon was erected in the 1960s. It celebrates the Portuguese explorers of the 1400s.

La Mezquita, Córdoba, Spain

During the early AD700s *Spain was conquered by the Moors from North Africa. The spectacular mosque in Córdoba with its colonnades and striped archways dates from that time.*

Portuguese cooper

A cooper (barrel maker) cuts staves for the big wooden barrels used to store port, a sweet after-dinner wine.

Velez-Blanco

The castle of Velez-Blanco crowns a rugged hilltop in Andalucia, southern Spain. It was built in the 1500s by Italians.

Andorra and Gibraltar

Most people in the tiny mountainous country of Andorra live in the valley of the Valira River. They process tobacco, graze sheep, or grow potatoes. Others work in the tourist trade. Andorra also makes money by selling inexpensive goods in low-tax stores, and by the sale of stamps. Native Andorrans are descended from a people called Catalans, who have their own language. Most non-Catalans speak Spanish.

Gibraltar is no more than a limestone rock, but it has strategic importance because it juts out towards Africa at the neck of the Mediterranean Sea. Britain seized Gibraltar from Spain in the 1700s and it remains a British colony and naval base. The land frontier between Gibraltar and Spain was reopened in 1983. Most people on Gibraltar work at the naval base or in the tourist industry.

Strange rock formations

A pillar of eroded rock shimmers in the summer heat on the edge of the Meseta, Spain's central plateau.

Italy and its neighbors

AUSTRIA

SWITZERLAND

Alps

Bolzano
▲ Mt. Ortles
12,812 ft.

Udine

SLOVENIA

Trieste

▲ Mt. Blanc
15,771 ft.

Bergamo

Piave

Milan   Brescia

Verona

Ticino

Padua

Venice

FRANCE

Oglio

Po

Turin

Tanaro

▲ Mt. Viso
12,602 ft.

Parma

Reno

Modena

Ferrara

Ravenna

CROATIA

Genoa

Bologna

La Spezia

Rimini

MONACO

San Marino

Apennines

SAN MARINO

Ligurian Sea

Pisa

Arno

Florence

Ancona

Adriatic Sea

Livorno

Perugia

Bastia

Elba

Tiber

Terni

Pescara

CORSICA
(France)

Ajaccio

ROME

Bonifacio

VATICAN
CITY

ITALY

Foggia

Ofanto

Sassari

Mt. Vesuvius ▲
4,000 ft.

Naples

Potenza

Salerno

Tar

Tirso

Sen

Oristano

Tyrrhenian Sea

SARDINIA
(Italy)

Cagliari

Cosenza

0   50   100   150   200   250   Kilometers
0   50   100   150   Miles

Lipari
Islands

Cata

Palermo

Messina

Reggio di
Calabria

Trapani

▲ Mt. Etna
10,900 ft.

N

SICILY
(Italy)

Catania

Agrigento

Syracuse

Mediterranean Sea

MALTA

■ Valletta

84

Italy is a peninsula that sticks into the Mediterranean Sea like a boot. The country also includes Sicily, Sardinia, and a number of smaller islands. Vatican City State and San Marino are two tiny independent countries within the Italian mainland. The Republic of Malta, a British colony from 1814 to 1964, consists of two Mediterranean islands, Malta and Gozo.

Italy enjoys mild, damp winters, but its hills and mountains can be cold and snowy. The summers are warm, with the southern and coastal plains becoming extremely hot and dusty. Regional differences in Italy are very strong, in everything from food to local customs. The way of life in wealthy northern cities such as Milan, Turin,

Venice

● ● ● ● ● ● ● ● ● ● ● ● ● ● ● ● ● ● ● ●

A vaporetto (water bus) chugs past the church of Santa Maria della Salute on Venice's Grand Canal. Venice is a city of canals where everyone travels by boat.

Bologna, and Genoa is also very different from that of poor farming communities of the south and Sicily.

Most Italians live in towns or cities, working mainly in service and manufacturing industries. Only nine percent still work in agriculture and in rural areas many farmhouses have been turned into vacation homes.

Sardinia

● ● ● ● ● ● ● ● ● ● ● ● ● ● ● ● ● ● ● ●

Masked riders take part in a horse race called the sartiglia *during the annual carnival in Oristano, on Sardinia's west coast.*

ndisi

History

Two thousand years ago this land was the heart of the Roman empire. It ruled much of Western Europe as well as territories all round the Mediterranean Sea. The Romans' language, Latin, is at the root of several modern European languages, including Italian and French. The influence of Roman architecture, laws, literature, and road building is still felt right across Europe today.

The Roman empire collapsed in AD476. The Italian peninsula split into a collection of cities and small states, although the city of Rome remained powerful as the center of the Roman Catholic Church. In the Middle Ages many of the independent cities grew wealthy through trade and banking, and also promoted art and science during the Renaissance, a time when new ideas swept through Europe.

From the 1500s some parts of Italy were ruled by France, Spain and Austria. Others were controlled by the Pope. Italy finally threw off foreign rule and united as an independent kingdom in 1861. In 1922 a fascist dictator, Benito Mussolini, came to power. He led Italy into World War II. Since 1947 Italy has been a democratic republic and a major industrial country.

The Leaning Tower of Pisa

* *

Pisa's leaning bell tower (1360s) was built of marble on sinking ground. Engineering work stops it from collapsing.

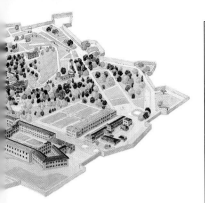

Vatican City

• • • • • • • • • • • • • • • • • • • •

Vatican City, the world's smallest country, lies within the city of Rome. It is the headquarters of the Catholic Church, headed by the Pope. Its main buildings are St. Peter's Basilica and the Papal Palace.

Economy

Italy is the world's leading wine-maker. It is also a major producer of olives and olive oil. Northern Italy has become one of the richest and most advanced industrial areas of Europe, hosting major international trade fairs as well as manufacturing automobiles, chemicals, and textiles. Milan is famous for fashion and Italian clothes, shoes, and leather goods are exported all over the world.

Goods for export overseas pass through the major ports of Genoa and Trieste. Italy has a large fleet of merchant ships as well as many fishing fleets, which catch tuna and sardines in the Mediterranean Sea. Over half of Italy's trade is with member states of the European Union. However, service industries such as tourism now generate more income than manufacturing.

■ **ITALY**
Area: 115,820 sq. mi.
Population: 57,057,000
Capital: Rome (2,724,000)
Official language: Italian
Currency: Italian lira
Main exports: Wine, machinery, transportation equipment, footwear, clothes, olive oil, textiles, mineral products

■ **SAN MARINO**
Area: 23 sq. mi.
Population: 23,000
Capital: San Marino (4,500)
Official language: Italian
Currency: Italian lira
Main exports: Wine, machinery, chemicals

■ **VATICAN CITY**
Area: 0.15 sq. mi.
Population: about 1,000

■ **MALTA**
Area: 119 sq. mi.
Population: 361,000
Capital: Valletta (102,000)
Official languages: Maltese, English
Currency: Maltese lira
Main exports: Machinery, clothes, textiles, transportation equipment, ships, beverages, tobacco

Maltese harbor

• •

A fisherman mends his nets in Malta's Marsa harbor. The picturesque town is a popular destination for tourists.

Poland and its neighbors

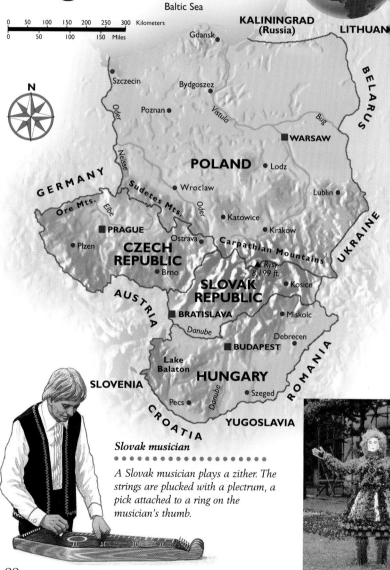

Baltic Sea

KALININGRAD
(Russia)

LITHUAN

0 50 100 150 200 250 300 Kilometers
0 50 100 150 Miles

Gdansk

Szczecin

Bydgoszcz

N

Oder

Poznan

Vistula

Bug

BELARUS

WARSAW

POLAND • Lodz

Neisse

GERMANY

Sudetes Mts.

• Wroclaw

Oder

Lublin

Ore Mts.

Elbe

• Katowice

• Krakow

PRAGUE

Ostrava

Carpathian Mountains

UKRAINE

• Plzen

**CZECH
REPUBLIC**

• Brno

▲ Rysy
8,199 ft.

**SLOVAK
REPUBLIC**

• Kosice

AUSTRIA

BRATISLAVA

• Miskolc

Danube

Debrecen

BUDAPEST

Lake
Balaton

HUNGARY

SLOVENIA

Danube

Pecs •

• Szeged

ROMANIA

CROATIA

YUGOSLAVIA

Slovak musician
••••••••••••••••••

*A Slovak musician plays a zither. The
strings are plucked with a plectrum, a
pick attached to a ring on the
musician's thumb.*

Much of Poland is covered by the vast open plains and rolling hills that stretch eastwards from Germany and on into Russia. Potatoes and rye are grown in the plains of central Poland. The most fertile land, on the hills of the south, produces wheat and corn. Cattle and sheep graze the southern pastures. In the far south of the country are forested mountains, which are home to bears and wolves. The Baltic coastal region to the north has thousands of lakes connected by rivers and streams and is dotted with peat bogs. Many Poles spend their leisure time in this area, windsurfing, fishing, yachting, and canoeing.

The Poles are a Slavic people who founded a powerful state in central Europe in the AD800s. From the 1300s to the 1600s this state became the center of a great empire. The empire declined and was divided between Russia, Prussia, and Austria in 1795. Independence was won back in 1918, but during World War II Poland was overrun by the Soviet Union and Nazi Germany.

Cesky Krumlov

The town of Cesky Krumlov stands amid wooded hills in the Czech Republic. It was founded in the 1200s and many of its buildings date from the Middle Ages. It became wealthy through silver mining.

Toward democracy

Nazi rule was brutal and millions of Poles were murdered. From 1947 Poland was governed by communists. During the 1970s and 1980s workers protested against bad living conditions with strikes and riots, demanding better pay and political reform. In 1989 democratic elections were won by Solidarity, the popular workers' party. The changeover from communism to democracy increased people's freedom, but at first it also brought widespread unemployment and high prices.

Up until the 1940s Poland's economy was based mainly on agriculture and most people lived and worked in rural areas. Today the majority live in cities. They work in service industries such as healthcare, education, and finance, or in heavy industries producing coal, steel, and machinery.

Polish floral statues

These floral statues represent figures from Polish folklore. During the communist era Polish traditions were suppressed. Today Poles are free to celebrate their national identity.

Hungary

Hungary's farmland is its chief resource. Crops of corn, wheat, potatoes, and sugar beet thrive in its rich black soil. Grapes and other fruit are grown for making wine and jams for export. Most farms are family collectives.

Communists took over the Hungarian government in 1948 and began a program of intensive industrialization. They restricted personal freedom and controlled wages and prices. When the Hungarians revolted in 1956, tanks rolled in from the communist Soviet Union to support the government and crush the rebellion. Many were killed or imprisoned. The government relaxed restrictions and democratic elections were held in 1990. Today most people live in cities and work in factories or service industries. The government is working to clean up industrial pollution left by the communist era.

Czech Republic

The Czech Republic is a country of fertile plains, wooded hills, and rugged mountains.

In 1918 the Czechs joined with their neighbors, the Slovaks, to form a new country called Czechoslovakia. From 1948 it was governed by communists, supported by the Soviet Union. The Czechoslovak communists demanded political reform in 1968, but their protest was squashed by Soviet troops.

Goulash
* * * * * * * * * * * * * * * * * * * *
Goulash is Hungary's national dish. It is a rich stew made with meat and potatoes and flavored with paprika and sour cream. Goulash is served with noodles and black bread.

Poland's capital
* * * * * * * * * * * * * * * * * * * *
Poland's capital, Warsaw, is a center of finance and administration. Heavy industries were set up here during the communist era when all factories were owned by the state. Today they are returning to private ownership.

Prague, Czech Republic

● ● ● ● ● ● ● ● ● ● ● ● ● ● ● ● ● ● ●

A series of bridges spans the broad Vltava River in the beautiful, old city of Prague, the capital of the Czech Republic. Prague has been a rich commercial center since the Middle Ages.

Slovakia

Slovakia is a land of mountains, lakes, and forests. The country was created in 1993 when Czechoslovakia split into two separate states. At first Slovakia faced economic problems because it had little manufacturing industry. Slovakia's natural resources are timber, iron ore, and the rich farmland around the river Danube, where farmers grow cereal crops and rear pigs. Around 40 percent of Slovaks work in industry, many producing consumer goods.

Then in 1989 a general strike triggered democratic elections. In 1993 Czechoslovakia was peacefully divided into two new independent countries—the Czech Republic and Slovakia. The Czech Republic includes former Czechoslovakia's industrial areas. Its factories produce steel, glass, machinery, paper, and beer.

■ **POLAND**
Area: 120,194 sq. mi.
Population: 38,459,000
Capital: Warsaw (1,655,000)
Official language: Polish
Currency: Zloty
Main exports: Copper, coal, machinery, vehicles, footwear

■ **SLOVAKIA**
Area: 18,850 sq. mi.
Population: 5,318,000
Capital: Bratislava (441,000)
Official language: Slovak
Currency: Koruna
Main exports: Iron ore, chemicals, petroleum products, steel, weapons

■ **CZECH REPUBLIC**
Area: 30,314 sq. mi.
Population: 10,328,000
Capital: Prague (1,215,000)
Official language: Czech
Currency: Koruna
Main exports: Machinery, transport equipment, chemicals, iron, steel

■ **HUNGARY**
Area: 35,760 sq. mi.
Population: 10,294,000
Capital: Budapest (2,000,000)
Official language: Hungarian
Currency: Forint
Main exports: Consumer goods, raw materials, agricultural products, machinery, transport equipment

Poland

Hungary

Czech Republic

Slovakia

91

The Balkans and Romania

AUSTRIA
SLOVENIA
Ljubljana ■
Zagreb ■
CROATIA
HUNGARY
UKRAINE
MOLDOVA
ROMANIA
Carpathians
Transylvanian Alps
Bucharest ■

BOSNIA-HERZEGOVINA
Sarajevo ■
Belgrade ■
Danube

YUGOSLAVIA
BULGARIA
Sofia ■
Black

Adriatic Sea
Skopje ■
MACEDONIA
Tirane ■
TURKEY

N

ALBANIA
GREECE
Thessaloniki ●

Aegean Sea

| 0 | 100 | 200 | 300 | 400 | Kilometers |
| 0 | 50 | 100 | 150 | 200 | 250 | Miles |

Pindus Mts.

Athens ●
Peloponnesus
Kalamai ●
Rhode

Khania ●
Iráklion ●
Crete

Greek statue

This statue of a discus thrower dates from 450BC. Discus throwing was one of the main events at the Olympic Games, which began in Greece in 776BC.

This area takes its name from the Balkan Mountains of Bulgaria. In these eight countries craggy mountains that are difficult to cross separate various groups of people with different languages, customs, and religions. Over the centuries these isolated communities have often fought for each other's territory.

The spectacularly rugged Adriatic coast is fringed with mountainous islands. Crops such as corn, fruit, and tobacco are grown along the coast and in the fertile plains of the Danube Basin. Tourism is an important source of income across the whole area. In the former Yugoslavia huge efforts are being made to restore historic towns and cities and to rebuild homes and factories devastated by war.

Macedonian church

The church of St. John at Caneo overlooks beautiful Lake Ohrid. Christianity is the main religion in Macedonia, but there are also many Muslims here.

A land of many islands

Greece occupies the southern part of the Balkan Peninsula. It includes hundreds of beautiful islands scattered in the deep blue Aegean and Ionian seas. The largest island is Crete, which lies farther south in the Mediterranean Sea. Greece has natural harbors, mountains and deep valleys. It is a rocky land of limestone covered in scrub and scented wild herbs grazed by flocks of sheep and goats. The earth is carpeted with flowers in spring but baked brown and dusty during the hot summer months. Olive groves and wheatfields surround peaceful whitewashed villages. However, Greece's cities, with their mix of ancient and modern buildings, are busy with people and traffic. Air pollution from automobiles and factories in Athens is threatening health and eating away at the many national monuments.

Greek salad

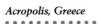

Greek salad is made with tomatoes, onions, cucumber, black olives, and cubes of feta cheese. It is sprinkled with herbs and olive oil. Crusty bread and a Greek wine called retsina often accompany this dish.

Acropolis, Greece

The Acropolis is a rocky fortress on a hill above Athens. The Parthenon, on its highest point, is a temple built in 438BC.

93

History

The first great European civilization began in Greece in about 2500BC. The ancient Greeks developed the idea of democracy, or rule by the people. Since the fall of the Greek empire, these lands have come under the rule of the Roman empire, Austria-Hungary and the Ottoman empire. After World War II much of the area fell under communist rule.

Communism collapsed in 1990 and Yugoslavia, which was a union of six republics including Croatia, Bosnia and Serbia, broke up into separate nations. When Croatia and Bosnia declared independence in 1991 and 1992 the Serbs living in those countries objected and began a brutal civil war. Thousands were killed or forced to flee their homes. Peace talks led to the Dayton Accord of 1995. Under this agreement, Bosnia-Herzegovina now consists of a Croat-Muslim province and a Serb province.

Economy

Under communist rule, which affected all these countries

Roman amphitheater

• •

The huge amphitheater at Pula in Croatia was built by the Romans in AD80. People came here to watch gladiators and wild animals fighting to the death.

except Greece, businesses and farms were taken into state ownership. The communists built many factories, but most people lived in rural areas where poverty was common. Today two thirds of the people live in cities. Many work in industry or tourism. The seafaring nation of Greece has important shipping and fishing industries. Rich deposits of iron, oil, and natural gas have brought new wealth to Albania.

Dalmatian pelican

• • • • • • • • • • • • • • • •

Dalmatian pelicans can be seen fishing in the delta of the Danube River on the Black Sea coast. Drainage of wetland and hunting have reduced their numbers.

Albanian apples

• •

Women sort apples at a factory at Peshkepi, in eastern Albania. Fresh fruit, canned fruit, jams, and juices are important to the Albanian economy.

ROMANIA

Area: 91,295 sq. mi.
Population: 22,755,000
Capital: Bucharest (2,351,000)
Official language: Romanian
Currency: Leu
Main exports: Petroleum products, oilfield equipment, cement

GREECE

Area: 50,725 sq. mi.
Population: 10,350,000
Capital: Athens (3,097,000)
Official language: Greek
Currency: Drachma
Main exports: Clothes, olive oil, petroleum products, fruit, tobacco

BULGARIA

Area: 42,665 sq. mi.
Population: 8,469,000
Capital: Sofia (1,142,000)
Official language: Bulgarian
Currency: Lev
Main exports: Machinery, food, wine, tobacco, fuels, and raw materials

ALBANIA

Area: 11,051 sq. mi.
Population: 3,338,000
Capital: Tirane (251,000)
Official language: Albanian
Currency: Lek
Main exports: Iron ore, natural gas, oil, chrome, bitumen, nickel, copper

SLOVENIA

Area: 7,784 sq. mi.
Population: 1,990,000
Capital: Ljubljana (268,000)
Official language: Slovenian
Currency: Tolar
Main exports: Machinery, transportation equipment, raw materials, food

CROATIA

Area: 21,734 sq. mi.
Population: 4,789,000
Capital: Zagreb (727,000)
Official language: Serbo-Croatian
Currency: Kuna
Main exports: Chemicals, clothes, food, machinery

BOSNIA-HERZEGOVINA

Area: 19,654 sq. mi.
Population: 4,366,000
Capital: Sarajevo (526,000)
Official language: Serbo-Croatian
Currency: Dinar
Main exports: Clothes, chemicals, furniture, machinery

MACEDONIA

Area: 9,883 sq. mi.
Population: 2,173,000
Capital: Skopje (449,000)
Official language: Macedonian
Currency: Denar
Main exports: Chemicals, clothes, footwear, machinery, transportation equipment, food, textiles

YUGOSLAVIA

Area: 32,274 sq. mi.
Population: 10,485,000
Capital: Belgrade (1,169,000)
Official language: Serbo-Croatian
Currency: Dinar
Main exports: Textiles, chemicals, clothes, food, iron, steel, machinery, transportation equipment, manufactured goods

Romania Croatia Greece Slovenia Macedonia

Bulgaria Yugoslavia Bosnia-Herzegovina Albania

Russia and its neighbors

ARCTIC OCEAN

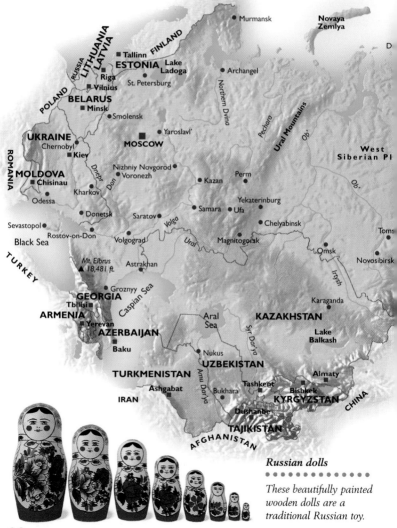

- Murmansk
- Novaya Zemlya
- D

LITHUANIA
LATVIA
FINLAND
RUSSIA
POLAND
- Tallinn
- ESTONIA
- Lake Ladoga
- Riga
- Vilnius
- St. Petersburg
- Archangel
- Northern Dvina

BELARUS
- Minsk
- Smolensk
- Yaroslavl'

Pechora
Ural Mountains
Ob'

West Siberian Pl

UKRAINE
- Chernobyl
- Kiev
- MOSCOW
- Nizhniy Novgorod
- Voronezh
- Kazan
- Perm
- Yekaterinburg
- Ufa

ROMANIA
MOLDOVA
- Chisinau
- Kharkov
- Don
- Dnepr
- Samara

- Odessa
- Donetsk
- Saratov
- Volga
- Chelyabinsk
- Magnitogorsk
- Toms

- Sevastopol
- Rostov-on-Don
- Volgograd
- Ural
- Omsk
- Novosibirsk

Black Sea

- Mt. Elbrus ▲ 18,481 ft.
- Astrakhan
- Irtysh

TURKEY

GEORGIA
- Groznyy
- Tbilisi
- Caspian Sea
- Karaganda

ARMENIA
- Yerevan
- AZERBAIJAN
- Baku
- Aral Sea
- Syr Dar'ya

KAZAKHSTAN
- Lake Balkash

- Nukus
- UZBEKISTAN
- Almaty

TURKMENISTAN
- Ashgabat
- Amu Dar'ya
- Bukhara
- Tashkent
- Bishkek
- KYRGYZSTAN

IRAN
- Dushanbe
- TAJIKISTAN

AFGHANISTAN

CHINA

Russian dolls

These beautifully painted wooden dolls are a traditional Russian toy.

96

N

| 0 | 250 | 500 | 750 | 1000 | Kilometers |
| 0 | | 250 | 500 | | 750 | Miles |

New Siberian Islands

ernaya mlya

Anadyr'

Bering Sea

Kolyma

RUSSIA

Indigirka

Verkhoyansk Range

Lena

Central Siberian Plateau

East Siberian Uplands

Yakutsk

izhnyaya Tunguska

Kamchatka Peninsula

Magadan

Sea of Okhotsk

Kuril Islands

Lena

Sakhalin

era

rasnoyarsk

Amur

Khabarovsk

Irkutsk

Lake Baikal

CHINA

Ulan-Ude

enisey

MONGOLIA

Vladivostok

JAPAN

Russian trawler

The catch taken by this Russian trawler is frozen on board ready for delivery to a fish processing factory. Fishing is an important part of the Russian economy. Both fresh and preserved fish are favorite foods of the Russian people.

Russia is the largest country in the world. It covers over 6 million square miles, borders 14 other countries, and crosses eight time zones. Extending north to the frozen wastes that lie above the Arctic Circle, its expanses also take in vast forests, high mountains, and wide plains. Russia has long bitter winters and short summers. Snow can cover more than half the country for six months a year, so it can be difficult to make the most of the many natural resources available. These resources include large regions of farmland and plentiful reserves of timber, oil, coal, and natural gas. The bitter cold means that few people live in the north, part of an area called Siberia. Political prisoners used to be sent to Siberian labor camps.

Borscht
• • • • • • • • • • • •
Borscht is a classic Russian soup and can be eaten hot or cold. It has beet as its main ingredient.

Revolution
For centuries Russia was a vast empire ruled by emperors called czars. The czars kept working people living in poverty so the upper classes could live in luxury. From the 1600s to the 1800s the workers' discontent with the czars erupted into revolts. By the early 1900s revolutionary groups had emerged and in 1917 a group called the Bolsheviks led a revolution under Lenin. Czar Nicholas II was killed and Lenin set up a communist government, forming the Union of Soviet Socialist Republics (U.S.S.R.).

Collapse of communism
Lenin's successor, Joseph Stalin, ruled by terror from 1929 until 1953. The 1940s to the 1980s marked a period of distrust between the West and communist countries in the East, which is often called the Cold War. When Mikhail Gorbachev became president in the 1980s he introduced reforms that gave the people greater freedom. At this time some republics began to demand independence. By the early 1990s communism had collapsed and most republics were independent.

Cotton harvest
• •
Cotton, harvested from the fields of Bokhara in Uzbekistan, is piled into fluffy heaps ready for sorting, processing, and weaving into fabric. Cotton is Uzbekistan's most important export.

Geography

Most of the area on the map lies in the Asian continent, but western Russia, Moldova, Belarus, Ukraine, and the Baltic States lie in Europe. The Ural Mountains are usually considered to divide Europe and Asia.

The Russian climate includes great extremes, growing hotter toward the south and colder and drier toward the east and north. Tundra covers much of the most northerly region. Little grows on this frozen plain and few people live there. Below this region a belt of dense forest sprawls across the land. Taiga (coniferous forest) covers the northern part of the belt. The soil is mainly too poor to grow crops. Farther south the forest becomes mixed coniferous and deciduous trees. The climate here is milder and some areas can be farmed.

Rolling plains known as steppes start below the forests. The Caucasus Mountains and the Caspian Sea form Russia's southernmost area. The slopes of the Caucasus Mountains have lush, green, fertile meadows, while the Urals contain important deposits of iron and copper.

Kalta Minar mosque, Uzbekistan

This tiled minaret was intended to be the tallest in Central Asia, but building stopped when ruler Mohammed Khan died in 1855.

Grain harvest

Combine harvesters work the fields on a government-owned Russian farm. Russia's vast areas of farmland make it one of the world's major grain producers.

A Polish Roman Catholic church rises against the skyline in Minsk, the capital of Belarus. Very few old buildings remain in the city, which was badly damaged during World War II.

Communist economy

When communism ended with the breakup of the Soviet Union in 1991, the newly independent states had to make the huge and very difficult change in their economy from communism to capitalism. The word *soviet* means a council elected by the people and the basis of communism was that everybody should share both the work and the profits. Communist law stated that the government of the Soviet Union owned all the country's factories and farms as well as controlling wages and prices. Any profits were shared by the people and no one was allowed to run a private business. From the 1920s onward the Soviet Union became a heavily industrialized nation. The government set up factories and mines all over the country. Huge state farms were created and farming practices were modernized with the use of pesticides and fertilizers to increase yields.

Toward capitalism

After communism collapsed government price controls were lifted. Under capitalism, producers could charge what they liked for goods, and prices soared. However, incomes remained very low and this caused severe economic problems. Shortages were just as common as they had been under communism, because ordinary people could not afford to pay for goods. Today economic hardship continues and shoppers jostle each other to buy food on the black (illegal) market. Heavy industry, farming, and mining still form the backbone of the economy and new ways are being found to exploit mineral resources.

100

The Russian people

The majority of Russians are descended from a people called Slavs, but there are small numbers of about 100 other ethnic groups. Most Russians live in European Russia, in the west of the country. Inuits are among the groups in the frozen far north. People in different areas feel strongly about their own identity. Some former Russian republics became independent in 1991 and there are still people in other parts of Russia who would like to break away from the mother state. One such area is Chechnya, with its capital at Groznyy, where a revolt broke out in 1994.

Three quarters of the population lives in towns and cities. Russian cities have huge populations, so many people live in crowded high-rise apartment buildings. Moscow has one of the highest population counts in the world—over eight million people have made their homes here.

During the years of communism education was made a top priority by the government, but religious worship and freedom of speech were severely restricted. With the end of communism Russian believers began to worship more openly.

Russia's strong artistic tradition has produced many famous writers, composers, artists, and musicians. From the 1800s onward the country was a world leader in literature, music, drama, ballet, and other arts. It has also become a leading medal-winner in the world of sport. This is actively encouraged by the government, which provides a wide range of sports facilities such as stadiums.

Ukrainian nuclear power station

The world's worst nuclear accident occurred in Chernobyl, north of Kiev, Ukraine, in 1986. Since then, many Ukrainians have opposed the use of nuclear power.

Moldova

Moldovans dress in traditional costumes to celebrate their country's independence in 1991. Moldovan customs and traditions were suppressed under communist rule.

The western states

Ukraine, Moldova, and Belarus lie in Europe. They gained independence in 1991 after the collapse of the Soviet Union. Now they belong to the Commonwealth of Independent States, an alliance of former Soviet states.

These countries have wide plains, forested hills, and many rivers. Fertile black soil covers much of the area, which has warm summers and mild winters. This makes the land suitable for farming and agriculture is very important to the economy. Crops include sunflowers (for vegetable oil), corn, wheat, tobacco, and root vegetables. Fruits are grown for the canning industry and vineyards produce wine. Food processing is a major industry. Other industries include the manufacture of cement, machinery, and clothes.

The Baltic states

Latvia, Lithuania, and Estonia lie on the coast of the Baltic Sea in Europe. During the communist era many Baltic nationals were sent to labor camps in Siberia. Their languages and customs were suppressed. The Soviet Union took farms into state ownership and set up factories. Heavy industry has caused serious environmental damage. The Baltic states declared independence in 1991 when communism collapsed.

These are countries of low forested hills, lakes, and streams. Crops include cereals, flax and potatoes. Cattle and pigs are also raised. Most people, however, live in cities and work in industry.

Dancers in Kazakhstan
• •
Dancers wearing traditional costume perform to singing or the recital of an epic poem. They relive a heroic story from Kazakhstan's past.

St. Anne's Church and the Church of the Bernardines are in Vilnius, Lithuania's capital. Religion was suppressed during the communist era. Today nearly all Lithuanians are Roman Catholics.

Armenia

Armenia is a rugged country in the Little Caucasus Mountains, with deep gorges, lakes, and rushing rivers. Between the 1890s and the end of World War I the Turks massacred more than half a million Armenians and others were deported or fled. Over the years people from Armenia have settled in many other countries, including Israel. Today there are millions of Armenians living all over the world.

Most Armenians were farmers or herders until their country came under Soviet rule. The Soviets set up copper mines and factories and many Armenians moved to the cities to work. Today only a third of the population is rural, keeping sheep or cattle and growing fruit and vegetables. Most people speak the Armenian language, which is unlike any other and has its own alphabet. The country also has a strong artistic tradition that includes religious music and the making of decorative stone carvings called *khatchkars*.

Georgia

Forested mountains cover much of this land. The coastal lowlands have a mild climate and plenty of rain. Farmers grow citrus fruits, tea, and tobacco. Farther inland cereals and vegetables are grown, as well as grapes for Georgia's famous wines. Georgia is noted for its food and hospitality and for the health resorts along its Black Sea coast. More than half the people live in cities and many work in food processing, the country's main industry.

Georgian horsemen

Georgian horsemen play a form of polo known as tskhenburi. Polo is a popular sport and most towns in Georgia sponsor a polo team.

103

Turkmenistan

Few people live in the arid desert region of Karakum that covers most of Turkmenistan. The inhabited areas of the country are mainly along the foothills of the Kopet Mountains in the south and in the river valleys in the southeast. Half the population of Turkmenistan makes its living from farming, which would be impossible without the canals that bring water from the rivers to irrigate the land. The most important crop is cotton, but grain, potatoes, and grapes are also grown. Thoroughbred Turkomen horses and karakul sheep are reared and some farmers also breed silkworms. Wool is woven into the highly colorful carpets for which the country is famous.

Azerbaijan

In Azerbaijan the lofty Caucasus Mountains sweep down to the Caspian Sea. In the southwest a corridor of Armenian territory separates one section of Azerbaijan, called Nakhichevan, from the rest. Much of the land is mountainous and through the broad valleys run the Kura and Aras Rivers, which provide

Tashkent
• • • • • • • • • • •

The soaring modern television tower dominates the skyline of Tashkent, the capital of Uzbekistan. The city of Tashkent has always been a major crossroads and center of communication and stands on the ancient Silk Road from China to the Middle East.

hydroelectric power for industry and irrigation for farming.

Azerbaijan was part of the Soviet Union until the Union broke up in 1991. The Russians brought heavy industry to the country and today the economy is based on Azerbaijan's large reserves of oil and natural gas. There are also many factories and over half the people live and work in towns and cities. In rural areas farmers grow cotton, fruit, tobacco, and tea. Sheep and goats are herded on the mountain slopes.

Ownership of the Nagorno-Karabakh region has been challenged by neighboring Armenia and there has been bitter fighting since the late 1980s.

Market in Tajikistan
• • • • • • • • • • • • • • • • • • •

At an open market in Tajikistan shoppers buy melons grown in the fierce summer heat. The men wear traditional embroidered skullcaps.

104

Uzbekistan

Much of Uzbekistan is a land of rolling plains and barren deserts, with the huge desert of Kyzylkum at its center. Streams flowing from Kyrgyzstan's mighty Tian Shan Mountains water the fertile, heavily populated valley that contains the town of Fergana.

Uzbeks are nomadic herders by tradition, but the Soviet Union turned much of the country's grazing land into cotton plantations and the Uzbeks began to work on these. Uzbekistan became independent when the Soviet Union broke up in 1991.

Kazakhstan

Kazakhstan stretches from the salty Caspian Sea to the soaring Altai Mountains. In the north are high grassy plains called steppes and in the south there are sandy deserts. Kazakhstan has bitter winters and long hot summers.

For centuries the Kazakhs were nomads, roaming the plains with their herds of camels, horses, sheep, and cattle. This traditional way of life changed when Russia conquered Kazakhstan about 100 years ago. The Russians began to mine iron and lead. They also planted the Kazakhs' grazing lands with wheat. When Kazakhstan became part of the Soviet Union rapid industrialization took place.

Many people in rural areas still live without electricity or running water. However, the discovery of oil in the Caspian Sea promises wealth. Independence in 1991 brought new pride in Kazakh traditions.

Turkmen carpet

A Turkmen woman works at the loom, weaving a carpet. Turkmen carpets have bold colors and a strong design.

Tajikistan

Tajikistan is a mountainous country, prone to earthquakes. In the Pamir Mountains snow makes the few roads impassable for more than six months a year. Yet in the fertile river valleys, where most people live, the summers are long and hot. Villagers grow mainly cotton, grain, vegetables, olives, figs, and citrus fruits. Cattle breeding is important on the rich pasture lands. More and more rural people are moving to cities to find jobs in Tajikistan's textile factories, steel works, and other industries.

Tajikistan was controlled by the Soviet Union from the 1920s. The Soviets built roads and schools, putting industry and agriculture under state control and discouraging religion. Independence came in 1991.

105

Estonia

● ● ● ● ● ● ● ● ● ● ● ● ● ● ● ● ● ● ● ●

Crowds of Estonians celebrate independence from the Soviet Union in 1991. They have gathered in Tallinn, their country's capital.

Kyrgyzstan

The early settlers of this mountainous country were nomadic peoples, who reared animals in the high valleys and took them down to graze in the warmer foothills during the bitterly cold winter months. Today only about half the population is rural, herding sheep, cattle, goats, and pigs or growing cotton and tobacco. Most rural people are ethnic Kyrgyz and live in large clans, each with its own leader. A minority live in *yurts*. These wooden-framed, felt tents are traditional Kyrgyz homes, but today there might be a modern car parked outside them. One fifth of the people live in cities and work in industry.

Russia took over this country in the 1870s, bringing farm workers into the region. This left the nomads with fewer grazing grounds. Kyrgyzstan gained independence in 1991.

■ **RUSSIA**
Area: 6,563,784 sq. mi.
Population: 148,366,000
Capital: Moscow (8,957,000)
Official language: Russian
Currency: Rouble
Main exports: Natural gas, petroleum, chemicals, machinery, timber, coal

■ **GEORGIA**
Area: 26,793 sq. mi.
Population: 5,471,000
Capital: Tbilisi (1,283,000)
Official language: Georgian
Currency: Lary
Main exports: Food, chemicals, machinery, metal products

■ **ARMENIA**
Area: 11,455 sq. mi.
Population: 3,732,000
Capital: Yerevan (1,283,000)
Official language: Armenian
Currency: Dram
Main exports: Chemicals, food products, machinery, metal goods

■ **AZERBAIJAN**
Area: 33,289 sq. mi.
Population: 7,392,000
Capital: Baku (1,081,000)
Official language: Azeri
Currency: Manat
Main exports: Chemicals, food, machinery, oilfield equipment, petroleum, natual gas, textiles

■ **KAZAKHSTAN**
Area: 1,044,530 sq. mi.
Population: 16,956,000
Capital: Almaty (1,151,000)
Official language: Kazakh
Currency: Tenge
Main exports: Oil, metals, chemicals, grain, wool

Georgia   Armenia

Kyrgyzstan   Latvia

■ TURKMENISTAN
Area: 187,626 sq. mi.
Population: 3,809,000
Capital: Ashgabat (411,000)
Official language: Turkmen
Currency: Manat
Main exports: Consumer goods, food, machinery, metals, oil, natural gas, cotton, textiles, chemicals

■ UZBEKISTAN
Area: 171,981 sq. mi.
Population: 21,207,000
Capital: Tashkent (2,120,000)
Official language: Uzbek
Currency: Som
Main exports: Cotton, chemicals, food, metals, minerals, machinery, textiles

■ TAJIKISTAN
Area: 55,000 sq. mi.
Population: 5,514,000
Capital: Dushanbe (592,000)
Official language: Tajik
Currency: Rouble
Main exports: Cotton, food, metals, textiles, fruit, vegetables

■ KYRGYZSTAN
Area: 76,303 sq. mi.
Population: 4,528,000
Capital: Bishkek (642,000)
Currency: Som
Official language: Kyrgyz
Main exports: Food, machinery, manufactured goods, wool, chemicals

■ LATVIA
Area: 24,490 sq. mi.
Population: 2,586,000
Capital: Riga (911,000)
Official language: Latvian
Currency: Lats
Main exports: Food, chemicals, manufactured goods

■ LITHUANIA
Area: 25,100 sq. mi.
Population: 3,730,000
Capital: Vilnius (593,000)
Official language: Lithuanian
Currency: Litas
Main exports: Food, chemicals, manufactured goods

■ ESTONIA
Area: 17,300 sq. mi.
Population: 1,517,000
Capital: Tallinn (503,000)
Official language: Estonian
Currency: Kroon
Main exports: Food, chemicals, manufactured goods

■ UKRAINE
Area: 232,100 sq. mi.
Population: 52,179,000
Capital: Kiev (2,651,000)
Official language: Ukrainian
Currency: Hryvna
Main exports: Metals, machinery, food, chemicals, textiles

■ MOLDOVA
Area: 13,000 sq. mi.
Population: 4,356,000
Capital: Chisinau (753,000)
Official language: Moldovan
Currency: Leu
Main exports: Chemicals, food, wine, machinery, textiles, tobacco

■ BELARUS
Area: 79,800 sq. mi.
Population: 10,313,000
Capital: Minsk (1,634,000)
Official language: Belarussian, Russian
Currency: Rouble
Main exports: Food, machinery, natural gas, transportation equipment, petroleum, chemicals, petrochemicals

Azerbaijan   Kazakhstan   Turkmenistan   Uzbekistan   Tajikistan

Lithuania   Estonia   Ukraine   Moldova   Belarus

ASIA

Some of the world's first great civilizations sprang up in Asia from 3500BC onward. Their riches attracted trade and conquering armies. Over the centuries peoples such as the Mongols and the Turks built up and then lost vast empires. From the 1800s much of Asia was colonized by European countries. These new rulers took away wealth, but did not help the colonies develop. The original inhabitants stayed poor and were denied good education and job opportunities.

Tipu's tiger

This model of a tiger eating a European was made for Tipu Sultan of Mysore, India, in the late 1700s.

Great social changes have taken place in Asia during this century. Many colonies, such as India and Jordan, have become independent nations. In countries where a large majority of poor people were ruled by a wealthy few, communism seemed to be the answer. However, the spread of communism often caused war with capitalist countries. In 1991 the Soviet Union abandoned communism and, as it broke up, republics such as Kazakhstan and Uzbekistan became independent countries. Some Asian countries still have communist governments, although a number have recently held democratic elections for the first time.

Many Asian governments are now improving the economies of their countries by creating new industries and improving old ones. They are using both government money and foreign aid.

■ CONTINENTAL FACTS
Area: 17,062,000 sq. mi.
Population: 3,381,282,000 (excluding Russia)
Independent countries: 48
Highest point: Mount Everest (29,028 ft.), world's highest peak
Lowest point: Shore of the Dead Sea (1,289 ft. below sea level), world's lowest point
Largest lake: Caspian Sea (143,250 sq. mi.)
Longest rivers: Yenisey (3,435 mi.), Yangtze (3,430 mi.), Ob (2,995 mi.), Hwang Ho (2,995 mi.)

Russian women
●●●●●●●●●●●●

In Siberia these Yakut
and Khant women are
making traditional
clothes. Today these are
worn only by rural
people on special
occasions.

Turkish mosaic
●●●●●●●●●●●●●●

This portrait of the
Emperor Justinian is
made of mosaic (colored
glass cubes set in plaster).
Justinian ruled the
Byzantine empire during
the AD500s. He made fair
laws and promoted arts
and learning.

China and its neighbors

RUSSIA

ULAN BATOR

MONGOLIA

KAZAKHSTAN

Altai Mountains

• Urümqi

Gobi Desert

Baotou ●

KYRGYZSTAN

Taiy

Huang He

TAJIKISTAN

Taklimakan
Desert

Altun Mts.

PAKISTAN

Kunlun Mountains

CHINA

Lanzhou ●

Tibetan
Plateau

Chengdu ●

Chongqing ●

INDIA

Chang Jiang Yr.

▲ Mt. Everest
29,028 ft

● Lhasa

Guiyang ●

NEPAL

BHUTAN

Mts. Kunming ●

Xi

MYANMAR
(Burma)

VIETNA

LAOS

Giant panda
● ●

*The giant panda lives in China's
southwestern bamboo forests. Its future is
threatened by the loss of this habitat and
by poaching. Efforts to breed giant pandas
in captivity in zoos around the world have
not proved successful.*

0	200	400	600	800	1000	1200	Kilometers
0		200		400		600	Miles

110

Khabarovsk
Qiqihar
Harbin
Changchun
ngyang
NORTH
KOREA
Pyongyang
JAPAN
NG
Lüda
Tianjin
Seoul
Zibo
SOUTH
KOREA
n
Qingdao
gzhou
Yellow Sea
Nanjing
Shanghai
Hangzhou
Wuhan
nangsha
Fuzhou
T'ai-pei
ngzhou
TAIWAN
Hong Kong
Macao
nan
and

N

China occupies about one fifth of the Asian continent. This colossal country has the largest population in the world. Every day about 50,000 babies are born here. In order to provide food for such large numbers of people, every scrap of fertile land has to be cultivated. China currently produces enough food for everyone to eat, but there will soon be too many people to feed.

The river valleys of eastern China have been farmed for thousands of years and great industrial cities have grown up in this region. Fewer people live in the remote areas of the north and west, where there are barren deserts and high mountains.

In modern times the narrow streets and low houses of China's major cities have been replaced with highways and skyscrapers. In contrast, life has hardly altered for centuries in rural areas. Most people are farmers and use traditional methods to cultivate rice on the terraced paddies.

Chinese dragon

A dragon is carried through the streets to the sound of exploding firecrackers during Chinese New Year celebrations. This festival is also celebrated in many overseas cities where people of Chinese descent have settled.

111

People and history

China has one of the world's greatest and most ancient civilizations, with a written history that stretches back more than 3,500 years. Among its many inventions are the compass, fine porcelain, silk, gunpowder, paper, printing, and even banknotes.

During this century, China has experienced many changes.

After more than 2,000 years as an empire, the country became a republic in 1911. Following an uprising in 1949, China became a communist state. Since then the standard of living for most people has risen. Industrial modernization has continued and services such as up-to-date telecommunications networks have been developed.

■ CHINA
Area: 3,679,822 sq. mi.
Population: 1,205,181,000
Capital: Beijing (7,500,000)
Official language: Mandarin
Currency: Yuan
Main exports: Crude oil, textiles, coal, grains, canned food, tea, fish products, raw silk, tungsten ore

■ TAIWAN
Area: 13,910 sq. mi.
Population: 20,800,000
Capital: Taipei (2,720,000)
Official language: Mandarin
Currency: Taiwan dollar
Main exports: Electrical equipment, machinery, textiles, metal goods, plastic goods

■ MONGOLIA
Area: 1,602,160 sq. mi.
Population: 2,371,000
Capital: Ulan Bator (575,000)
Official language: Mongolian
Currency: Tugrik
Main exports: Minerals, meat, hides, wool, livestock, consumer goods

■ NORTH KOREA
Area: 47,190 sq. mi.
Population: 23,054,000
Capital: Pyongyang (2,640,000)
Official language: Korean
Currency: Won
Main exports: Coal, iron, copper, textiles

■ SOUTH KOREA
Area: 38,160 sq. mi.
Population: 44,056,000
Capital: Seoul (10,628,000)
Official language: Korean
Currency: Won
Main exports: Machinery, electronic and transport equipment, manufactured goods, textiles, steel

■ MACAO
Area: 6.5 sq. mi.
Population: 388,000
Capital: Macao
Official languages: Portuguese, Cantonese
Currency: Pataka
Main exports: Clothing, textiles, toys

■ HONG KONG
Area: 1,414 sq. mi.
Population: 5,919,000
Status: This prosperous former British dependency will become a Special Administration Region of China on July 1, 1997

Hong Kong

China

Taiwan

Mongolia

North Korea

South Korea

The junk is a traditional Chinese boat. It has a high poop, a flat bottom and a square sails supported by battens.

dry to grow crops without irrigation. Also, expanding cities and factories have tended to spread across precious farmland. The people of China provide a large work force, but as the population continues to grow more resources are needed for food, healthcare, and education.

Towards a free market

China's farmers and workers had suffered centuries of injustice and poverty when the communists came to power in 1949 and attempted to improve their lives. In the 1950s and 1960s heavy industry was developed under state control. Farming was organized in communes, where villagers combined their land and farmed it together. From the 1980s free markets and private ownership were allowed in some areas. The economy boomed and Chinese goods were soon flooding all over the world.

Natural resources

China has rich resources of coal, oil, iron, tungsten, timber, hydroelectric power, and fisheries. It is the world leader in rice and tobacco and its fertile farmland also produces large quantities of other crops including sorghum and wheat. It also has a centuries-old tradition of commerce, craft skills, and invention. Despite all these advantages, the country has always had economic problems and still does today.

Many of its minerals are found only in remote, inaccessible regions. There are large areas of barren wilderness where it is too

Terra-cotta army

The tomb of Emperor Shi Huangdi, who died in 210 B.C., was guarded by an army of soldiers made out of terra-cotta.

113

N. and S. Korea—history

North Korea and South Korea formed a single country for hundreds of years, from the 1300s until this century. Between 1910 and 1945 Korea was occupied by Japan. This ended when Japan was defeated in World War II. After this the country divided into two, with U.S. troops occupying southern Korea and Soviet Union troops occupying the north. In 1950 North Korea attacked South Korea and millions were killed or made homeless. The war ended in 1953, but tensions between North and South Korea have continued.

N. and S. Korea—economy

North Korea is a communist country where all the factories, farms, even the cars, are owned by the government. The farms are collectives, where work and profits are shared. Most workers have jobs in factories. They ride bicycles to work, leaving their babies in state-run nurseries.

South Korea has one of the world's fastest-growing economies. Its industry is highly developed, producing computers and electrical goods. The country's rapid industrial growth has taken place since 1950. Before this its economy was based on farming. South Korea is a capitalist country. Its industry is privately owned.

Taiwan

Taiwan is an island off mainland China. One third of Taiwan's workers have jobs in manufacturing and it exports goods all over the world.

In the past, the island has been ruled by both Japan and China. In 1949, when China became communist, its defeated leaders fled to Taiwan and set up a government there. Tensions remain between anticommunist Taiwan and China.

Horse racing
• • • • • • • • •
Boys and girls as young as five take part in horse racing in Mongolia. Jockeys usually retire around age 12.

114

Hong Kong

Hong Kong was loaned to Britain by China in 1842. It has become an important center for trade, manufacturing, and finance. Hong Kong was returned to China in 1997.

Mongolia

In the Middle Ages Mongolia built up one of the largest empires the world has ever seen under the leadership of Genghis Khan. When the empire fragmented, Mongolia was swallowed up by China. In 1924 it became a communist republic under the influence of the Soviet Union. Since the breakup of the Soviet Union in 1991, Mongolia has been a democracy.

By tradition Mongolians are herders. Mounted on stocky ponies, they cross the country's bleak landscape of sand and gravel in seach of pasture for their sheep. Today, many have settled to work on livestock farms. Others have jobs in factories or mining.

Communist workers

There are many statues of heroic communist workers in North Korea. Since the country became communist in 1948 it has become heavily industrialized.

Macao

This view from Penha Hill shows the fourteenth-century temple, Ma Kwok, from which the colony takes its name.

115

Japan

Soya

Buddhist temple
. . . .
*Daigo-Ji is a Buddhist
temple in the ancient city of
Kyoto. Built of wood in the
traditional Japanese style, it
is set in a beautiful garden.*

■ JAPAN
Area: 145,200 sq. mi.
Population: 124,959,000
Capital: Tokyo (7,976,000)
Official language: Japanese
Currency: Yen
Main exports: Machinery, vehicles,
ships, electronic equipment, steel,
chemicals, textiles

Asa

Otaru
Sapporo

Hakodate

Ac

Hachir

Akita M

Honsh

Sea of Japan

Yamagata

Niigata

Koriyama

Kanazawa
Toyama
Utsunomiya
Shinano Abukuma

Takasaki
Mi

JAPAN
TOKYO ■ Chiba
Mt. Fuji ▲ Yokohama
12,388 ft.

Nagoya

Matsue
Kyoto
Okayama Kobe Shizuoka
Hiroshima Osaka Hamamatsu
Takamatsu Sakai
Matsuyama Tokushima Wakayama

Kitakyushu
Fukuoka
Kochi
Oita **Shikoku**
Nagasaki
Kumamoto
Kyushu
Miyazaki
Kagoshima

NORTH PACIFIC
OCEAN

N

0   100   200   300   400 Kilometers
0   100   200 Miles

116

Tokyo Tower
• • • • • • • • •

*Tokyo Tower, built in
1958 to broadcast
radio and television,
sparkles against the
night sky. At 1,092 ft.
it is the tallest structure
in Japan's capital city.*

The Japanese call their island country Nippon, meaning "the source of the sun." This ancient name explains the red disk on their national flag, which represents the rising sun. For many centuries emperors have been heads of state in Japan. Until 1946 Japanese emperors claimed to be divine, believing they were descended from the gods. Today the emperor's role and duties are ceremonial only. Modern Japan is world famous for its powerful business corporations and advanced electronics technology. However, this is still a land in which traditions and ancient customs are held in the highest respect. Among the busy streets and bright lights of the capital visitors can glimpse the past in the form of temples and shrines. They can also take part in *chanoyu,* a 500-year-old tea-drinking ceremony that honors courtesy and hospitality.

Most of the population lives in crowded cities on the coastal plains. Inland are forested hills and mountains. The land is both beautiful and unstable. There are many volcanoes and earthquakes are common throughout Japan.

Kabuki *players*
• • • • • • • • • • • •

*Actors in traditional
costume and makeup
perform a Japanese kabuki
play. Men play both male
and female roles and act
out stories to music.*

117

Economy

Japan is a land of economic miracles in both agriculture and industry. The country has only a small area of farmland, but yields of rice, tea, fruit, and other crops are high. This is thanks to modern farming methods, which include growing specially developed high-yield crops and using fertilizers and pesticides. Modern equipment also means that fewer people are needed to work the land.

These small islands have become one of the world's greatest industrial powers. They have achieved this with hard work and investment in new technology. Japan has to import huge amounts of oil and raw material for industry, but it produces more automobiles and color televisions than any other country. Japanese firms have expanded to open factories all over the world.

Large companies demand great loyalty from their staff. Employees may be expected to sing a special company song, wear a company uniform, and join in daily physical exercise sessions. In return, many employers organize their workers' vacations, healthcare, and housing.

Sushi

Sushi is a favorite snack food in Japan. Slices of very fresh raw fish or shrimp and pickled vegetable wrapped in seaweed are beautifully presented on little mounds of rice.

Golf in Tokyo

Players practice their swing in a three-level golf driving range in Japan's capital. Tokyo is densely populated with little open space, but this does not deter its golfers.

Decorated boats take to the sea during a Japanese fishing festival. The fleet follows to give thanks for their catch.

History

The Middle Ages was a time of turmoil. Power passed from a long line of emperors to warlords called shoguns. Sometimes there were civil wars between rival bands of warriors called samurai. From 1603 to 1867 Japan was united under shogun rule and closed its doors to the outside world. Then the emperors returned to power and opened up the country. A period of rapid industrialization followed.

During the 1930s the Japanese army invaded China. Then, during World War II, it overran most of Southeast Asia and the Pacific islands. Japan was defeated in World War II and occupied by U.S. forces until 1952. Since the 1950s the war-damaged economy has grown rapidly and today Japan is a major world economic power.

Geography

Japan is made up of about 3,000 islands. They are the tops of a huge mountain range that rises from the Pacific Ocean. Its rocks are still on the move, and sometimes this causes volcanic eruptions, earthquakes, or huge waves called *tsunamis*.

Most Japanese live on the four largest islands, even though much of the land is taken up by towering mountains and forested hills. Streams and waterfalls tumble through deep gorges in this spectacular landscape.

On the coastal lowlands some of the most crowded cities on Earth spread on to land reclaimed from the sea.

Tokyo fish market

A woman buys octopus in Tokyo. Japan is a leading fishing nation and most Japanese eat fish every day.

Southeast Asia

N

| 0 | 250 | 500 | 750 Kilometers |
| 0 | 100 | 200 | 300 | 400 | Miles |

CHINA

Red

MYANMAR
(Burma)

Hanoi ■ • Haiphong

Chiang Mai •

LAOS

■ Vientiane

THAILAND

Bangkok ■

Da Nang •

Mekong

CAMBODIA

VIETNAM

Phnom Penh •

• Nha Trang

• Ho Chi Minh City

Gulf of
Thailand

South China Sea

Luzon

■ Manila

PHILIPPI

Cebu

Sulu Sea

Minda

Zamboanga •

Ipoh

MALAYSIA

Medan •

■ Kuala Lumpur

Bandar Seri Begawan

BRUNEI

**EASTERN
MALAYSIA**

B o r n e o

Celebes Sea

SINGAPORE

Batanghari

Pontianak •

Kapuas

Padang •

Sumatra

• Jambi

Palembang •

Balikpapan •

Barito

**Sulawesi
(Celebes)**

Banjarmasin •

Java Sea

Ujung Pandang •

Jakarta ■

I
N
D
O
N
E
S
I
A

Bandung • **Java** Surabaya

Malang • **Bali**

Flores

Javanese puppets

Javanese puppets are made of painted
leather. The puppeteer moves them with
rods and wires to enact the
traditional folk tales of Java.

Timor Sea

Southeast Asia has forested mountains, broad river valleys, low plains, and palm-fringed beaches. Its tropical climate, fertile soil, and plentiful monsoon rains make it ideal rice-growing country. The economy depends largely on agriculture. Most people live in villages, many in houses built on stilts, and work in the paddy-fields. Manufacturing industries thrive in the cities. The tiny nation of Brunei has become vastly wealthy since oil was discovered here in the 1920s.

All these countries except Thailand were once part of European empires. The Europeans established rubber, copra, palm oil, and banana plantations and developed the trade in spices. During this century the colonies gained independence, but this did not always bring peace. Many countries fell under military rule and oppression continues today.

Vietnam, Cambodia, and Laos were involved in a major war. The French ruled Vietnam until 1954, when communist guerrillas took over the north and the country was split into North Vietnam and South Vietnam. When communists tried to

Singapore

Singapore is an island republic linked by bridge to mainland Malaysia. The country's wealth is based on shipping, banking, electronics, and trade.

take over South Vietnam as well, North and South went to war. In 1965 the United States joined forces with the South against the communist North. Bitter fighting spilled over into Cambodia and Laos. The government of South Vietnam was overthrown in 1975. The U.S. troops left and the country became one again in 1976. Vietnam's economy and environment suffered greatly as a result of the war. However, much has been done to repair the damage. Tourism and trade have developed steadily.

imor

Sculpture park in Laos

Buddha Park near Vientiane, the capital of Laos, features many Hindu as well as Buddhist sculptures. The park was built to honor both religions and their philosophies.

Indonesian gamelan

A gamelan is a collection of Indonesian musical instruments. It may include up to 40 drums, gongs, xylophones, and chimes. Played together, they make a magical tinkling sound.

Indonesia

Indonesia is the world's biggest archipelago, a long chain of more than 13,600 mountainous islands. Their many active volcanoes form part of the danger zone that geologists call the Pacific Ring of Fire. Indonesia has seen some of the most violent volcanic eruptions ever recorded. However, people continue to live close to the smouldering volcanoes because their ash makes the soil rich and fertile. The economy is based on agriculture, forestry, and fishing.

Malaysia

Malaysia is a green land with mountains cloaked in dripping rain forest, huge plantations of rubber and oil palms, and sandy beaches. Many Malays work growing rice and pineapples. Along the coast most people fish for a living. A large Chinese minority (35 percent of the population) lives mainly in the cities. Malaysia has achieved economic success with rubber, tin, and oil. Timber-felling has laid waste great areas of forest, but is now government controlled.

Malaysian satay

Small pieces of meat are skewered and barbecued over glowing charcoal to make satay. The dish is served with rice and peanut sauce.

Philippines

This island nation has many active volcanoes. Much of the land is clad in forest. Under the dictatorship of President Marcos the country suffered corruption, pollution, and poverty. Marcos was overthrown in 1986. Today's government is working to solve the problems he left behind.

Rice terraces

The rice terraces of Luzon in the Philippines were dug out 2,000 years ago. Modern farming practices have increased rice production, but pesticides have damaged much of the land.

122

■ **BRUNEI**
Area: 2,920 sq. mi.
Population: 276,000
Capital: Bandar Seri Begawan
(46,000)
Official language: Malay
Currency: Bruneian dollar
Main exports: Crude oil, liquefied
natural gas, petroleum products

■ **SINGAPORE**
Area: 246 sq. mi.
Population: 2,874,000
Capital: Singapore City
Official languages: English, Mandarin,
Malay, Tamil
Currency: Singaporean dollar
Main exports: Machinery, vehicles,
electronic equipment, petroleum
products, rubber, chemicals, food,
clothes

■ **PHILIPPINES**
Area: 115,300 sq. mi.
Population: 65,649,000
Capital: Manila (1,599,000)
Official language: Filipino, English
Currency: Philippino peso
Main exports: Clothes, electronic
equipment, coconut oil, timber

■ **MALAYSIA**
Area: 126,690 sq. mi.
Population: 129,239,000
Capital: Kuala Lumpur (938,000)
Official language: Bahasa Malaysia
Currency: Malaysian dollar
Main exports: Rubber, palm oil,
timber, petroleum, tin, electronic
equipment

■ **INDONESIA**
Area: 737,830 sq. mi.
Population: 198,070,000
Capital: Jakarta (6,504,000)
Official language: Bahasa Indonesia
Currency: Rupiah
Main exports: Oil, liquefied natural
gas, timber, rubber, coffee

■ **CAMBODIA**
Area: 69,590 sq. mi.
Population: 9,308,000
Capital: Phnom Penh (800,000)
Official language: Khmer
Currency: Riel
Main exports: Rubber, rice, pepper,
timber

■ **LAOS**
Area: 91,429 sq. mi.
Population: 4,605,000
Capital: Vientiane (378,000)
Official language: Lao
Currency: Kip
Main exports: Timber, electricity,
coffee, tin

■ **VIETNAM**
Area: 91,030 sq. mi.
Population: 70,902,000
Capital: Hanoi (1,089,000)
Official language: Vietnamese
Currency: Dong
Main exports: Coal, iron, agricultural
products including rice, rubber

■ **THAILAND**
Area: 197,240 sq. mi.
Population: 58,584,000
Capital: Bangkok (5,876,000)
Official language: Thai
Currency: Baht
Main exports: Rice, tapioca,
manufactured goods, machinery

Brunei　　Singapore　　Philippines　　Malaysia　　Indonesia

Cambodia　　Laos　　Vietnam　　Thailand

India and its neighbors

Htamin le thoke

In Myanmar this dish consists of small helpings of leftovers such as rice, onions, potatoes, noodles, and spinach. It is served with tamarind juice.

Indian dancers

Traditional costume is worn for kathakali dancing in southwest India. The dancers tell stories about the lives of Hindu gods.

AFGHANISTAN

Herat
Mazar-e-Sharif
Hindu Kush
Kabul
Disputed Area
Qandahar
Islamabad
Rawalpindi
Srinagar
Rigestan Desert
Quetta
Lahore
Faisalabad
Amritsar
Multan
Ludhiana
PAKISTAN
Thar Desert
Gwadar
Sukkur
Indus
Nanda Devi 25,645 ft
CHINA (Tibet)
Himalayas
Delhi
NEW DELHI
NEPAL
Mt. Everest 29,028 ft
Karachi
Hyderabad
Jodhpur
Jaipur
Agra
Katmandu
Thimp[
Ajmer
Lucknow
Kanpur
Ganges
Brah
Allahabad
Patna
Varanasi
Ahmadabad
BANGLA[
Indore
Surat
INDIA
Jamshedpur
Dha
Calcutta
Chi
Nagpur
Bombay (Mumbai)
Deccan
Pune
Godavari
Cuttack
Sholapur
Eastern Ghats
Hyderabad
Vishakhapatnam
Hubli-Dharwar
Vijayawada
Western Ghats
Mangalore
Bangalore
Madras
Mysore
Calicut
Coimbatore
Cochin
Madurai
Jaffna
Trivandrum
Trincomalee
SRI LANKA
Colombo
Kandy
Galle

Indian well

• • • • • • • • • • • • • • • • • •

Women collect water for cooking and washing from a well in the desert of Rajasthan, India. They carry it home in pots made of metal or clay balanced on their heads.

India is a land of contrasts. There are mountain ranges hidden permanently under ice and snow, plains crossed by broad rivers, a parched desert, and tropical forests. Most Indians live in rural areas, where they grow rice and wheat and keep animals on small plots of land. Indian farms are getting smaller all the time, because under Hindu law, land is divided equally among the children on their parents' death.

In recent years thousands have moved to the cities to find work in industry. Heavy machinery and electrical goods are now manufactured alongside traditional products such as cotton and silk. Service industries such as tourism, education, and communications are also growing in importance, as is the thriving film industry based in Bombay.

Afghan girl

• • • • • • • • • • • • • • • • • • •

This Afghan girl wears brightly colored traditional dress and jewelry. She belongs to the Kyrgyz people of the far northeast.

Bangladeshi mothers

• • • • • • • • • • • • • • • • • • • •

A healthworker in Bangladesh holds a clinic for mothers and babies. She may also advise on nutrition and food preparation.

Hkakabo ▲
19,295 ft.

JTAN

phal

● Mandalay

MYANMAR
(Burma)

Irrawaddy

THAILAND

Moulmein

■ Yangon
(Rangoon)

N

| 0 | 250 | 500 | 750 Kilometers |
| 0 | 100 | 200 | 300 | 400 | 500 Miles |

125

India's people and history

India has many ethnic groups, languages, and religions. Most people are Hindu. According to Hindu tradition, people are born into social classes called castes. Strict rules govern the clothes, food, and jobs of each caste.

In rural areas the way of life has not changed for centuries. In the cities people live crowded together in slums, while wealthier Indians choose a Western lifestyle.

India has seen the rise and fall of great empires founded on Buddhism, Hinduism, and Islam. In 1858 India became part of the British empire. From the 1920s demands for self-rule grew with a peaceful campaign organized by

Pakistani potter
. . . .
A potter adds the finishing touches to a teapot in Peshawar, Pakistan. Pakistan has a long tradition of fine craftwork, which also includes carpet making, leather tooling, and metalwork.

126

Swedagon Pagoda
. . . .
Buddhist monks process toward this beautiful gilded temple in the capital of Myanmar, Yangon, formerly Rangoon.

Mahatma Gandhi. Independence finally came in 1947. Since then, the country has experienced conflicts over religion and language, but it has remained the world's largest democracy.

Afghanistan

Afghanistan has rugged, snow-capped mountains and scorching deserts. In summer, some Afghans roam the grasslands with their herds and sleep in tents of felted goat hair. In winter they settle to farm the valleys.

In the 1970s the Soviet Union became influential in Afghanistan and in 1979 Soviet troops invaded to support the left-wing government. Civil war then devastated the country. Soviet troops withdrew from Afghanistan in 1989, and in 1996 a Muslim group called Taliban (a word meaning "students") controlled most of the country.

■ MYANMAR (BURMA)
Area: 260,080 sq. mi.
Population: 44,613,000
Capital: Yangon (formerly Rangoon, 2,459,000)
Official language: Myanmar
Currency: Kyat
Main exports: Teak, rice, pulses, rubber

■ AFGHANISTAN
Area: 250,660 sq. mi.
Population: 20,547,000
Capital: Kabul (700,000)
Official languages: Pashto, Dari
Currency: Afghani
Main exports: Karakul skins, raw cotton, fruit and nuts, natural gas, carpets

■ INDIA
Area: 1,263,715 sq. mi.
Population: 913,600,000
Capital: Delhi (8,400,000)
Official languages: 16 including Hindi, Bengali, Gujarati, Urdu
Currency: Indian rupee
Main exports: Gems and jewelry, clothes, cotton, textiles, tea, engineering goods

■ PAKISTAN
Area: 306,020 sq. mi.
Population: 126,284,000
Capital: Islamabad (201,000)
Official language: Urdu
Currency: Pakistani rupee
Main exports: Cotton and cotton goods, rice, leather, carpets, fish

■ MALDIVES
Area: 115 sq. mi.
Population: 238,000
Capital: Male (56,000)
Official language: Divehi
Currency: Rufiyaa
Main export: Fish

■ SRI LANKA
Area: 25,220 sq. mi.
Population: 17,619,000
Capital: Colombo (588,000)
Official languages: Sinhalese, Tamil
Currency: Sri Lankan rupee
Main exports: Textiles, clothes, tea, gems, rubber, coconut products

■ BANGLADESH
Area: 57,040 sq. mi.
Population: 122,210,000
Capital: Dhaka (6,106,000)
Official language: Bengali
Currency: Taka
Main exports: Jute, tea, hides, clothes, leather, newsprint, fish

■ BHUTAN
Area: 17,870 sq. mi.
Population: 1,650,000
Capital: Thimphu (31,000)
Official languages: Dzongkha, English, Nepali
Currency: Ngultrum
Main exports: Timber and wood products, coal, rice, oranges and apples, distilled spirit, talc, cement

■ NEPAL
Area: 56,580 sq. mi.
Population: 21,086,000
Capital: Katmandu (419,000)
Official language: Nepali
Currency: Nepalese rupee
Main exports: Grains, jute, timber, oil seeds, clarified butter, potatoes, herbs, hides

Myanmar

Afghanistan

India

Pakistan

Maldives   Sri Lanka   Bangladesh   Bhutan   Nepal

Pakistan and Bangladesh

Pakistan was once part of the British empire. When India won independence from Britain in 1947, two separate Muslim areas in northwest and northeast India became the country of Pakistan. Muslims from all over India moved to the new country while most Hindus stayed in India. In 1971 civil war broke out between East and West Pakistan, which split into two countries. The eastern half renamed itself Bangladesh, while the western half became modern-day Pakistan.

North Pakistan is a beautiful land of lakes and mountains. In the south is a sandy desert. In the center is a great plain watered by the Indus River and its tributaries. A vast irrigation system allows the cultivation of wheat, rice, and sugarcane. Pakistan's many industries produce cotton, carpets, sugar, metalwork, and processed foods.

Most of Bangladesh is flat, very low-lying land. Two great rivers, the Ganges and the Jamuna, spill into a maze of waterways, forming the largest delta in the world. There are frequent floods, which have drowned livestock and people and washed away crops, causing famine. Most people live in villages and grow rice, sugarcane, and jute, which is used to make ropes and matting.

Nepalese statue
• • • • • • • • • • • •
This gilded statue of King Yoganendra Malla, a 17th-century ruler of Patan in Nepal, stands in Patan's Durbar Square. A cobra rises behind the king.

Afghani bus
• •

Open-topped trucks are used in Afghanistan for transporting people as well as goods. They are often beautifully painted and decorated by their owners.

Myanmar

Myanmar was called Burma until 1989. It is rimmed by mountains. Most people live in the delta of the Ayeyarwady (Irrawaddy) River and work in rice paddies.

After independence from Britain in 1948, the country fell under harsh military rule. Objectors were shot or gaoled. In 1990 an election was held. The opposition party won, but the military continued in power.

Indian Ocean islands

The Maldives are a string of about 1,200 tiny tropical islands lying southwest of India. They are low and flat, many only just sticking up above sea level. Southeast of India is Sri Lanka, a large island ringed with palm-fringed beaches. It has a fertile plain that rises through rolling hills to misty mountains. Rain forest covers the southwest. About half the population are farmers, producing coconuts, rubber, rice, and tea. A major source of the islanders' income is fishing, though tourism is the fastest-growing industry.

Himalayan countries

Nepal and Bhutan lie in the Himalaya Mountains. The world's highest peak is Mount Everest in Nepal. Long-haired oxen called yaks are herded in the mountains, but most people are arable farmers, growing barley, citrus fruits, and rice on the humid and fertile southern plains.

Tourism has boosted Nepal's economy, but it also threatens the environment. A cloud of pollution hangs over the capital, Katmandu. Trekkers and locals use timber for fuel and much of the country's forests have been cut down. Everyone is now encouraged to conserve resources.

In Bhutan, tourism and mountaineering are limited.

Bhutani farmhouses
● ●

In Bhutan traditional farmhouses cling to the mountainside above irrigated terraced fields. Villages are often isolated because they are cut off by the mountains.

Gathering sea salt
● ●

In India salt-gatherers build low walls to trap the seawater when the tide comes in. When the water evaporates in the sun, salt is left behind.

The Middle East

Iraq, Iran, and Kuwait have vast expanses of desert. However, the discovery of oil has brought great wealth to these countries. Disputes over oil rights have also led to war.

Iraq and Iran are Islamic countries, governed by strict religious laws that deny many personal freedoms. Under Saddam Hussein, who came to power in 1979, Iraq invaded Iran. They fought from 1980 until 1988 over the Shatt al Arab Waterway, the important oil route that divides the two countries. Thousands were killed. In 1990 Iraq invaded Kuwait and claimed its territory. In 1991 Allied forces, including troops from Britain and the United States, drove out the Iraqis. The Iraqis retaliated with bombs, setting hundreds of Kuwaiti oil wells on fire. Kuwait's economy was badly damaged and the land and sea polluted.

The Iraqi government has also persecuted the Kurds and the Marsh Arabs, many of whom have fled the country. Life is difficult for most other Iraqis because war has destroyed families, homes, and jobs. Sanctions imposed by the United Nations have harmed the economy.

Yemeni Arab

Curved daggers called djambias are carried by most Yemeni men. The daggers have ornately carved handles made of ivory.

Iranian oil wells

Gas jets flame and black smoke fills the desert sky over the oil wells at Marun in Iran. Pollution is caused as waste gases are burned off the oil.

Klaicha

. . . .

Klaicha *are small Iraqi pastries stuffed with dates and dusted with sugar. Date palms are widely grown in Iraq. Dates are also eaten in meat dishes.*

Mt Ararat ▲
17,011 ft.

ARMENIA

AZERBAIJAN

Aras

Tabriz

Caspian Sea

Rasht

TURKMENISTAN

Mosul

▲ Mt. Damavand
18,386 ft.

Mashhad

Kirkuk

TEHRAN ■

Tigris

Qom

AFGHANISTAN

Bakhtaran

Dasht-e Kavir

AQ

■ BAGHDAD

IRAN

Karbala

Esfahan

Zagros Mountains

Yazd

Dasht-e Lut

An Nasiriyah ●

Ahvaz ●

Al-Basrah ●

Abadan ●

Kerman

Zahedan

KUWAIT

Shiraz

■ Kuwait

Busehr ●

Persian Gulf

Bandar Abbas

An Nafud

Strait of Hormuz

Jask

Buraydah ●

BAHRAIN

■ Al Manamah

QATAR

Shaqra ●

■ Doha

Dubai ●

Gulf of Oman

■ RIYADH

■ Abu Dhabi

UNITED ARAB EMIRATES

■ MUSCAT

SAUDI ARABIA

Jabal Ash Sham
9,957 ft. ▲

● Sur

Arabian Sea

▲ Jabal Sawda
10,279 ft.

Rub al Khali
(Empty Quarter)

OMAN

N

● Salalah

INDIAN OCEAN

SAN'A

Hadhramaut

| 0 | 100 | 200 | 300 | 400 | 500 | 600 | Kilometers |

● Al Hudaydah

YEMEN

● Al Mukalla

| 0 | 100 | 200 | 300 | 400 | Miles |

● Aden

Gulf of Aden

Socotra (Yemen)

The Arabian Peninsula

The countries of the Arabian Peninsula are Saudi Arabia, Yemen, Kuwait, Qatar, United Arab Emirates, and Oman. Bahrain is an island nation linked to the mainland by a causeway. Most of the peninsula is a desert where years pass without rain. Its only inhabitants are the Bedouin, who move with their camels between oases. Along the coast, people live by fishing or diving for pearls.

However, life has changed dramatically with the discovery of oil. Today the majority live in cities and work in the petroleum and construction industries. Profits from oil have been used to build roads and desalination plants that turn seawater into fresh water. Major irrigation systems enable some desert land to be farmed. New industries such as plastics and fertilizers are being developed. Oil money also provides free healthcare and other services including education.

Turkey and Cyprus

Turkey was once the center of the mighty Ottoman empire, which lasted for 500 years, finally breaking up in 1920. Modern-day Turkey was established in 1923 by Mustafa Kemal. He abolished the Islamic legal system and gave women the vote.

In 1974 Turkey invaded Cyprus and forced the Greek Cypriots who lived in the north to flee to the south. The island remains divided, with continuing tension between Greek and Turkish Cypriots.

Fast food in Oman

● ●

A McDonald's sign advertises burgers at Muscat in Oman. Since the discovery of oil in the Middle East, Western corporations have rushed to sell their products to the Arab nations.

Krak des Chevaliers Castle, Syria

● ●

This castle was built by the Crusaders in the 1200s. The Crusaders were European Christians who tried to recapture the Holy Land (Palestine) from the Arabs.

Turkish Cypriots

● ●

Village men relax in the sun outside a café in the north of Cyprus. They are playing tavala (the Cypriot name for backgammon). This dice game originated in Turkey and is popular throughout Turkish (northern) Cyprus.

Lebanon

Some of the people of Lebanon are Palestinian Arabs who believe that lands owned by Israel are rightfully theirs. The Palestine Liberation Organization (PLO) has been in conflict with Israel for many years and between 1969 and 1991 used Lebanon as a base for attacks on Israel. The country's Muslims and Christians have also had long-standing political differences. These, combined with the Palestine–Israel dispute, led to the outbreak of civil war in 1975. Troops from both Syria and Israel became involved and fighting continued until 1991. Some Israeli and Syrian troops remained in Lebanon to protect their countries' interests.

Turkish women
• • • • • • • • • • • • • • •

These Turkish women are spinning wool using short sticks called spindles. The wool fibers are twisted together to make a strong yarn.

Jewish call to prayer
• • • • • • • • • • • •

The Jewish New Year festival of Rosh Hashanah begins with the blowing of a ram's horn. It calls people to make a new start and pray for past wrongs.

Israel

Israel is part of a historic land called Palestine. It was founded in 1948 as a home for the Jews. Since then, there have been bitter wars between the Jews and their Arab neighbors. The Arabs formed the Palestine Liberation Organization (PLO), believing that Israel's land belongs to them. In the 1960s Israel occupied Arab land on the Gaza Strip, the West Bank, the Golan Heights, and the Sinai Peninsula. In 1994 peace was agreed between Israel and the Arabs, but tension continued.

Jordanian harvest

● ●

Women pick the lettuce crop in the fertile valley of the river Jordan. The Middle East has little fertile land, but thanks to massive irrigation projects, some areas of desert can now be farmed.

Syria and Jordan

Syria and Jordan were two of the leaders of Arab opposition to their Jewish neighbor Israel. In 1967 Israel occupied Syria's territory in the Golan Heights, and the West Bank, formerly in Jordan.

Syria is undergoing rapid industrialization. Many people are moving to the towns in search of jobs in the developing textile and chemical industries. About half the people still live in farming villages along the coast, in the fertile river valleys, and on the grassy western plains, where they grow cotton, fruit, and vegetables.

Most Jordanians live in towns and cities. Many work for the government or in service industries such as finance, trade, and tourism. Much of the land is rock or desert, so there is little large-scale agriculture. However, vegetables and citrus fruits are grown in the Jordan River valley.

■ **CYPRUS**
Area: 3,550 sq. mi.
Population: 723,000
Capital: Nicosia (167,000)
Official languages: Greek, Turkish
Currency: Cyprus pound
Main exports: Clothes, shoes, wine, potatoes, citrus fruit

■ **TURKEY**
Area: 299,620 sq. mi.
Population: 58,775,000
Capital: Ankara (3,023,000)
Official language: Turkish
Currency: Turkish lira
Main exports: Textiles, iron, steel, tobacco, fruit, leather clothing

■ **SYRIA**
Area: 71,180 sq. mi.
Population: 13,393,000
Capital: Damascus (1,497,000)
Official language: Arabic
Currency: Syrian pound
Main exports: Petroleum and petroleum products, cotton, natural phosphate, fruit, and vegetables

■ **LEBANON**
Area: 4,020 sq. mi.
Population: 2,901,000
Capital: Beirut (1,500,000)
Official language: Arabic
Currency: Lebanese pound
Main exports: Clothes, jewelry, fruit

■ **ISRAEL**
Area: 8,440 sq. mi.
Population: 5,256,000
Capital: Jerusalem (557,000)
Official language: Hebrew, Arabic
Currency: Shekel
Main exports: Fruit, vegetables, oil products, chemical products

Turkey

Syria

Kuwait

Saudi Arabia

■ JORDAN
Area: 35,320 sq. mi.
Population: 4,440,000
Capital: Amman (1,272,000)
Official language: Arabic
Currency: Jordan dinar
Main exports: Phosphate, potash, fertilizers, fruit, and vegetables

■ IRAQ
Area: 168,490 sq. mi.
Population: 19,918,000
Capital: Baghdad (3,850,000)
Official language: Arabic
Currency: Iraqi dinar
Main exports: Petroleum, wool, dates

■ IRAN
Area: 633,490 sq. mi.
Population: 63,180,000
Capital: Tehran (6,043,000)
Official language: Farsi
Currency: Rial
Main exports: Petroleum, carpets, fruit, cotton, textiles, metalwork

■ KUWAIT
Area: 6,850 sq. mi.
Population: 1,433,000
Capital: Kuwait City (32,000)
Official language: Arabic
Currency: Kuwaiti dinar
Main export: Petroleum

■ SAUDI ARABIA
Area: 845,680 sq. mi.
Population: 16,472,000
Capital: Riyadh (1,500,000)
Official language: Arabic
Currency: Riyal
Main exports: Petroleum and petroleum products, wheat, dates

■ YEMEN
Area: 204,120 sq. mi.
Population: 12,302,000
Capital: San'a (500,000)
Official language: Arabic
Currency: Yemeni riyal
Main exports: Petroleum products, cotton, fish

■ OMAN
Area: 118,970 sq. mi.
Population: 1,697,000
Capital: Muscat (380,000)
Official language: Arabic
Currency: Omani rial
Main exports: Petroleum, fish

■ UNITED ARAB EMIRATES
Area: 32,160 sq. mi.
Population: 1,206,000
Capital: Abu Dhabi (363,000)
Official language: Arabic
Currency: Dirham
Main exports: Petroleum, natural gas, fish, dates

■ QATAR
Area: 4,400 sq. mi.
Population: 559,000
Capital: Doha (236,000)
Official language: Arabic
Currency: Qatari riyal
Main exports: Petroleum, fertilizers

■ BAHRAIN
Area: 265 sq. mi.
Population: 521,000
Capital: Al Manamah (152,000)
Official language: Arabic
Currency: Bahraini dinar
Main exports: Petroleum, aluminum products, manufactured goods, machinery, transportation equipment

Lebanon   Israel   Jordan   Iraq   Iran

Yemen   Oman   United Arab Emirates   Qatar   Bahrain

AFRICA

■ CONTINENTAL FACTS
Area: 11,654,600 sq. mi.
Population: 697,000,000
Independent countries: 53
Highest point: Mt. Kilimanjaro
  (19,340 ft.)
Lowest point: Lake Assal in Djibouti
  (508 ft. below sea level)
Largest lake: Lake Victoria
  (26,710 sq. mi.)
Longest rivers:
  Nile (4,135 mi.)
  Zaire (2,993 mi.)
  Niger (2,594 mi.)

The map of Africa shows over 50 countries. Just 50 years ago most were ruled by powerful European nations, which became rich from mining and farming their colonies. From the 1960s African nations began to regain independence. However, the years of foreign rule had left most Africans poor, and without education or training. Colonial rule had often set one people against another and traditional homelands had been divided by new national borders. Trying to unite nations where people spoke many different languages and followed different religions was a hard task.

Many countries suffered years of dictatorship and millions became refugees from war, drought, and famine. White South Africans refused to give the vote to the black people who made up most of this nation's population. However, in 1994 hope was brought to the continent when Nelson Mandela became South Africa's first black president. In the 1990s many African countries started holding democratic elections and looking toward a more peaceful future.

Berber waterseller

A familiar sight in Morocco, the waterseller offers cool drinks from his goatskin bag.

Yamoussoukro Cathedral

This 518 ft. high Roman Catholic cathedral is at Yamoussoukro in Côte d'Ivoire. The Basilica of Our Lady of Peace cost millions of dollars and was completed in 1989.

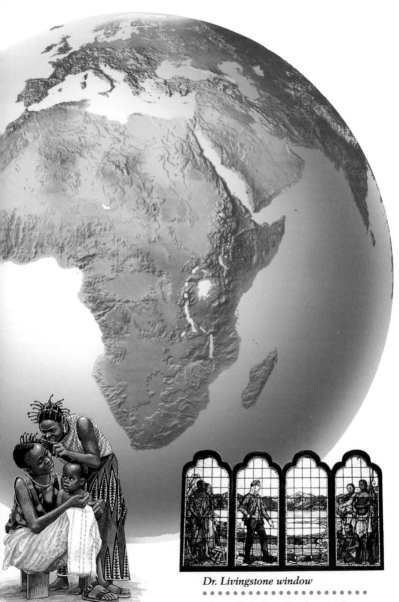

Zairean women

Zairean women weave each other's hair into many tiny braids, adding beads. These styles take hours to create.

Dr. Livingstone window

This cathedral window from Malawi celebrates Dr. David Livingstone, the famous Scottish missionary. He explored Malawi in the 1850s, campaigning against slavery.

North Africa

North Africa is mainly desert, yet around 200 million people live here. The people of the north are of mixed Berber and Arab descent. Arab conquerors invaded in the AD600s and converted the original Berber inhabitants to Islam. Over the centuries, the two peoples intermarried, but they still form separate cultural groups.

The eastern peoples of Egypt and Sudan are descended from Nubians and Arab traders who settled the region. One of the world's greatest civilizations developed in the Nile Valley. The Ancient Egyptians were brilliant architects and engineers who built huge temples, tombs, and towns. They studied the stars and worshipped many different gods. Their belief in life after death led them to preserve the bodies of their dead as mummies.

Powerful empires

The powerful Ghana, Mali, and Songhai empires flourished south of the Sahara during the Middle Ages. Their wealth came from trade in gold, ivory, and slaves.

Before independence around 50 years ago, most North African countries were controlled by France, and their people still speak French today. Morocco was controlled by France and Spain, Libya by Italy, Egypt by Britain, and Sudan by Britain and Egypt. Ethiopia, with one of the oldest civilizations in Africa, has always managed to hold on to its independence.

Mask of Tutankhamun
....

This is the gold mask of Tutankhamun, a young Egyptian pharaoh (king) who died around 1340BC. It was discovered by British archaeologists in 1922.

Map labels

SPAIN
Tangier
Oran
Rabat
Casablanca
MOROCCO
Marrakech
Atlas Mts.
Gharda
CANARY Is.
Ifni
ALGER
WESTERN SAHARA
In
S a
Mt. Tal 9,24
MAURITANIA
MALI
Ah
Nouakchott
Timbuktu
Sénégal
Kaédi
Niger
SENEGAL
Kayes
Ségou
Niamey
GUINEA
Bamako
BURKINA FASO
BENIN

N

0   250   500   750   1000 Kilometers
0 100 200 300 400 500 600 Miles

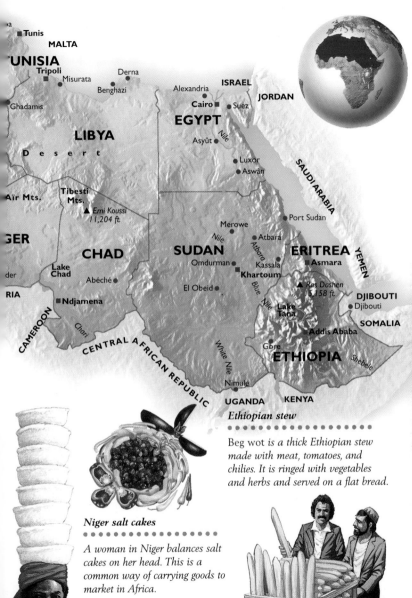

Tunis

MALTA

TUNISIA

Tripoli

Misurata

Derna

Benghazi

ISRAEL

Alexandria

JORDAN

Ghadamis

Cairo Suez

EGYPT

Nile

LIBYA

Asyût

D e s e r t

Luxor

Aswân

SAUDI ARABIA

Aïr Mts.

Tibesti Mts.

▲ Emi Koussi 11,204 ft.

Port Sudan

Merowe

Nile

Atbara

ERITREA

GER

CHAD

SUDAN

Atbara

YEMEN

Lake Chad

Abéché

Omdurman

Kassala

Asmara

der

RIA

Ndjamena

El Obeid

Khartoum

Blue

▲ Ras Dashen 15,158 ft.

DJIBOUTI

Nile

Djibouti

CAMEROON

Chari

Lake Tana

SOMALIA

CENTRAL AFRICAN REPUBLIC

White Nile

Gore

Addis Ababa

ETHIOPIA

Shebele

Nimule

UGANDA

KENYA

Ethiopian stew
. . . .

Beg wot *is a thick Ethiopian stew made with meat, tomatoes, and chilies. It is ringed with vegetables and herbs and served on a flat bread.*

Niger salt cakes
. . . .

A woman in Niger balances salt cakes on her head. This is a common way of carrying goods to market in Africa.

Algerian bread
. . . .

Algeria was once a French colony and Algerians still bake bread in the French style.

139

| Morocco | Western Sahara | Mauritania | Algeria | Tunisia |

■ MOROCCO
Area: 176,340 sq. mi.
Population: 26,069,000
Capital: Rabat (519,000)
Official language: Arabic
Currency: Dirham
Main exports:
Phosphates, fertilizers, mineral products, dates, figs, canned fish, tobacco

■ WESTERN SAHARA
Area: 96,910 sq. mi.
Population: 261,000

■ MAURITANIA
Area: 396,200 sq. mi.
Population: 2,206,000
Capital: Nouakchott
Official languages:
Arabic, French
Currency: Ouguiya
Main exports: Fish, iron ore, gypsum

■ ALGERIA
Area: 915,540 sq. mi.
Population: 27,070,000
Capital: Algiers (1,507,000)
Official language: Arabic
Currency: Algerian dinar
Main exports: Oil, natural gas, olive oil, wine, machinery

■ TUNISIA
Area: 63,100 sq. mi.
Population: 8,579,000
Capital: Tunis (597,000)
Official language: Arabic
Currency: Tunisian dinar
Main exports: Crude oil, fertilizers, phosphates, olive oil, textiles, fruit, fish products, machinery

■ LIBYA
Area: 676,370 sq. mi.
Population: 4,700,000
Capital: Tripoli (858,000)
Official language: Arabic
Currency: Libyan dinar
Main export: Petroleum

■ EGYPT
Area: 384,960 sq. mi.
Population: 56,488,000
Capital: Cairo (6,452,000)
Official language: Arabic
Currency: Egyptian pound
Main exports: Crude and refined oil, cotton, fruit

■ SUDAN
Area: 963,235 sq. mi.
Population: 28,129,000
Capital: Khartoum (477,000)
Official language: Arabic
Currency: Sudanese dinar
Main exports: Cotton, gum arabic, sesame seeds, peanuts, sorghum

■ CHAD
Area: 493,570 sq. mi.
Population: 6,098,000
Capital: N'Djamena (530,000)
Official languages:
Arabic, French
Currency: Franc CFA
Main exports: Cotton, livestock, meat, hides

■ NIGER
Area: 487,030 sq. mi.
Population: 8,361,000
Capital: Niamey (399,000)
Official language: French
Currency: Franc CFA
Main exports: Uranium, livestock, vegetables

■ MALI
Area: 476,730 sq. mi.
Population: 10,137,000
Capital: Bamako (740,000)
Official language: French
Currency: Franc CFA
Main exports: Cotton, livestock, peanuts

■ ETHIOPIA
Area: 444,980 sq. mi.
Population: 56,900,000
Capital: Addis Ababa (1,700,000)
Main language: Amharic
Currency: Ethiopian birr
Main exports: Coffee, hides, pulses, oil seeds

■ ERITREA
Area: 36,010 sq. mi.
Population: 3,500,000
Capital: Asmera (368,000)
Official language:
Currency: Ethiopian birr
Main exports: Hides, cement, salt, gum arabic, citrus fruit

| Libya | Egypt | Sudan |

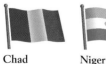

| Chad | Niger | Mali | Ethiopia | Eritrea |

Geography

North Africa is dominated by the world's largest desert, the Sahara. This scorching wilderness crossed by camel trains is bordered to the north by the fertile Mediterranean coast. In the northwest, the Atlas Mountains rise up, causing enough winter rain to grow crops such as wheat, grain, citrus fruit, and olives. To the south of the Sahara Desert is a hot, dusty region called the Sahel. Here, nomadic peoples herd their animals across the thin scrub in search of pasture. In the east, the river Nile, carrying water from central Africa, has provided a lifeline through the shifting sands of Egypt for thousands of years. The Nile has been dammed at Aswan to produce hydroelectric power. Beyond this great river in the southeast are the relatively cool mountains of the Ethiopian Highlands.

Libyan mosques
* * * * * * * * * * * * * * * * * * * *

Mosques rise above the skyline of Tripoli. Libya's capital has grown since the oil boom of the 1970s to house workers from the countryside.

Sudanese harvest
* * * * * * * * * * * * *

A woman sorts gum arabic into a basket. Gum arabic is produced by a type of acacia tree, and used in the manufacture of pills and paints.

Malian Muslims
* *

Traders and travelers collect outside the Great Mosque at Djenné. Most Malians are Muslims. Mali has been a center of Islam since AD1324.

Way of life

Many North Africans have moved to towns to work in factories or mines. Yet nomadic peoples such as the Bedouin and the Tuareg still live in the Sahara Desert by trading and herding camels and goats. They sleep in tents of animal hides. Some have settled at oases scattered across the desert. Farmers thrive along the Mediterranean coast, but others have been left starving and homeless by droughts that have made the land unproductive.

141

Economy

Libya has the richest economy in North Africa, based on its reserves of oil. The government has used profits from oil to improve farmland and to pipe water supplies across the desert. New industries have been developed, including mining and food processing. Mining boosts the economy in other North African countries, too. Oil and gas are mined in Algeria, phosphates in Tunisia and Morocco, iron ore and copper in Mauritania, and uranium in Niger.

Farming occupies little land but many people. Algeria and Tunisia produce citrus fruits and olives, cotton is a valuable export crop in Egypt, and coffee grows in the cool mountains of Ethiopia. Many North African farmers use wooden plows pulled by oxen to prepare the land for sorghum, teff, and corn, which are the main food grains. It is often a struggle to survive because of the severe droughts that plague these countries.

Tourism is increasingly important in Morocco, Tunisia, and Egypt. Visitors come to enjoy the sun and ancient monuments.

A ruined city in Algeria
• •

Ruined columns at Djemula, near Sétif, date back 2,000 years. At this time Algeria formed part of the fertile Roman province of Numidia.

Roman colosseum in Tunisia
• •

The ruined colosseum of El Jem is a reminder that Tunisia was once part of the Roman empire. Chariot races and savage fights were staged here.

Lake Chad
• •

Lake Chad is vital to the poor country of Chad. Camels that have traveled long distances across the desert can drink here and the deep waters are rich in fish.

142

The Suez Canal

The 100-mile Suez Canal was completed in 1869. It enables ships to pass directly from the Mediterranean Sea to the Gulf of Suez instead of sailing all the way around Africa. In 1956 Egypt's President Nasser nationalized the canal and as a result Egypt was attacked by Israel, Britain, and France. The canal was closed from 1967 to 1975 because of further wars with Israel. Today Egypt is enlarging the canal to take big oil tankers and boost its revenue.

Sudanese school
● ●

Schoolchildren in central Sudan listen attentively to their teacher. Education in the south of the country has been disrupted for decades because of the civil war between Muslims and Christians.

The Nile River

Nearly all Egyptians live on the narrow strip of land watered by the Nile River. This is the only fertile land in Egypt and covers less than six percent of its territory. Heavy rains at the source of the Blue Nile in Ethiopia make the river flood each year, leaving behind rich black mud ideal for growing crops. Since 1970, the floods have been controlled by the Aswan Dam, which produces hydroelectricity. However, the dam has also brought problems. The changes that it has made to the river's silt content have led to the erosion of the Mediterranean coast and to less fertile farmland.

Aswan High Dam, Egypt
● ●

The Aswan High Dam controls the floodwaters of the Nile. It has also silted up Lake Nasser, robbing farmland along the Nile of valuable nutrients.

143

West Africa

The culture of this region stretches back to the ancient empires of West Africa, such as Ghana, Mali, and Songhai, which thrived between the AD500s and the 1500s. As these empires declined, smaller, independent kingdoms grew up. Then in the 1400s Portuguese traders arrived, and were soon joined by the British, French, and Dutch. Over the next 400 years waves of Europeans invaded and set up colonies. They exploited the people and the land, establishing gold mines and plantations growing coffee, cocoa, sugar, and cotton, and forcing the Africans to work on them as slaves. They also shipped Africans out to the Americas, where they were sold as slaves to other plantation owners. Many Africans died on the way, or did not survive the harsh life of slavery.

African elephant

The African elephant has long been killed in large numbers so that its tusks can be taken for the ivory trade. Today it is an endangered species.

Toward democracy

Slavery, the cruel trade in human beings, was abolished by Britain in 1807, but independence was slow to come. The colonial powers did not leave West Africa until the mid-1900s. Since then, some countries have known periods of military rule and dictatorship. Colonialism left most West Africans without education or training. Conflicts often developed between ethnic groups. Today education is improving and many countries are now democracies.

Voodoo queens

Cameroon's voodoo queens, who practice traditional spells and healing, sway during a ritual dance. Belief in the spirit world is widespread in the countries of West Africa.

MAURITAN

SENEGAL
■ Dakar

GAMBIA
Banjul ■

Bissau ■

GUINEA-
BISSAU   GUIN

Conakry ■

Freetown ■
SIERRA LEONE

Monrovia ■
LIBE

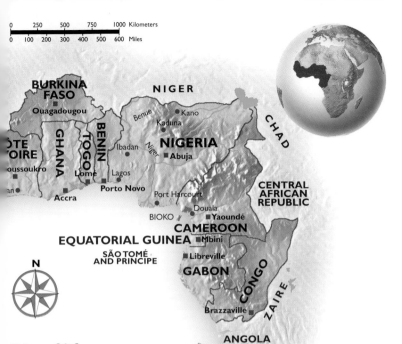

Way of life

In the towns of West Africa, people live in modern high-rise homes, or in wooden houses with tin roofs. Many townswomen travel to rural areas each day to work on small farms or help raising poultry or pigs. In the coastal lagoons villages of thatched huts are built on stilts in the water. The fishermen and traders who live there travel in canoes. Most West Africans live in mud huts in rural areas and are relatively poor farmers or herders. They grow millet, cassava, and rice for food. Cotton, peanuts, and palm oil are grown as cash crops. Some workers operate modern machinery on rubber plantations

Cotton plant

● ● ● ● ● ● ● ● ● ● ● ● ●

Cotton grows well in a tropical climate watered by heavy summer rain. The plants produce round bolls, which contain the soft white fibers used to make cotton fabric.

owned by foreign companies.

The harsh terrain and humid climate make farming difficult, yet the land holds priceless treasure. Nigeria is one of the world's major oil producers. Its oilfields are operated by foreign companies, which take about half the profits, with Nigeria receiving the remainder. Elsewhere in the region phosphates are mined for use in fertilizers. Huge deposits of diamonds, bauxite, and iron ore promise future wealth.

145

SENEGAL
Area: 75,790 sq. mi.
Population: 7,736,000
Capital: Dakar
(1,382,000)
Official language: French
Currency: Franc CFA
Main exports: Fish
products, peanuts,
phosphates, chemicals

GAMBIA
Area: 4,340 sq. mi.
Population: 1,026,000
Capital: Banjul (45,000)
Official language: English
Currency: Dalasi
Main exports: Peanuts
and peanut products,
fish and fish products,
hides, palm oil

CAPE VERDE ISLANDS
Area: 1,550 sq. mi.
Population: 395,000
Capital: Praia (62,000)
Official language:
Portuguese
Currency: Cape Verde
escudo
Main exports: Fish, salt,
bananas

GUINEA BISSAU
Area: 13,880 sq. mi.
Population: 1,028,000
Capital: Bissau (125,000)
Official language:
Portuguese
Currency: Guinea-Bissau
peso
Main exports: Fish,
peanuts, coconuts

GUINEA
Area: 94,510 sq. mi.
Population: 6,306,000
Capital: Conakry
(706,000)
Official language: French
Currency: Guinea franc
Main exports: Bauxite,
alumina, fruit, hides,
diamonds, coffee

SIERRA LEONE
Area: 28,170 sq. mi.
Population: 4,494,000
Capital: Freetown
Official language: English
Currency: Leone
Main exports: Bauxite,
rutile, cocoa, coffee,
diamonds, ginger

LIBERIA
Area: 38,080 sq. mi.
Population: 2,640,000
Capital: Monrovia
(425,000)
Official language: English
Currency: Liberian dollar
Main exports: Iron ore,
rubber, timber, coffee,
cocoa, palm oil,
diamonds, gold

CÔTE D'IVOIRE
Area: 123,960 sq. mi.
Population: 13,397,000
Capital: Yamoussoukro
(2,534,000)
Official language: French
Currency: Franc CFA
Main exports: Cocoa,
coffee, petroleum
products, timber, fruit

GHANA
Area: 91,690 sq. mi.
Population: 16,446,000
Capital: Accra (868,000)
Official language: English
Currency: Cedi
Main exports: Cocoa,
gold, timber, bauxite,
manganese, diamonds

TOGO
Area: 21,830 sq. mi.
Population: 3,885,000
Capital: Lomé (500,000)
Official language: French
Currency: Franc CFA
Main exports:
Phosphates, cotton,
coffee, cocoa

BENIN
Area: 43,290 sq. mi.
Population: 5,215,000
Capital: Porto-Novo
(209,000)
Official language: French
Currency: Franc CFA
Main exports: Petroleum,
cotton, cocoa, sugar,
palm oil, peanuts,
cement

BURKINA FASO
Area: 105,480 sq. mi.
Population: 9,682,000
Capital: Ouagadougou
(443,000)
Official language: French
Currency: Franc CFA
Main exports: Cotton,
karite nuts, livestock,
gold

NIGERIA
Area: 355,100 sq. mi.
Population: 119,328,000
Capital: Abuja (306,000)
Official language: English
Currency: Naira
Main exports: Petroleum,
cocoa, palm oil, rubber

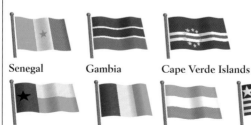

Senegal Gambia Cape Verde Islands

Guinea Bissau Guinea Sierre Leone Liberia Côte d'Ivoire

Ghana

■ CAMEROON
Area: 182,760 sq. mi.
Population: 12,547,000
Capital: Yaoundé
(750,000)
Official languages:
French, English
Currency: Franc CFA
Main exports: Crude oil,
timber, cocoa, coffee,
peanuts, bananas, cotton

Togo

■ EQUATORIAL
GUINEA
Area: 10,780 sq. mi.
Population: 379,000
Capital: Malabo (10,000)
Official language:
Spanish
Currency: Franc CFA
Main exports: Cocoa,
timber, coffee

Benin

■ SÃO TOMÉ AND
PRINCIPE
Area: 384 sq. mi.
Population: 122,000
Capital: São Tomé
(35,000)
Official language:
Portuguese
Currency: Dobra
Main exports: Cocoa,
copra, coffee, bananas,
palm oil

Burkina Faso

■ GABON
Area: 102,890 sq. mi.
Population: 1,012,000
Capital: Libreville
(350,000)
Official language: French
Currency: Franc CFA
Main exports: Oil,
manganese, timber,
uranium

Nigeria

■ CONGO
Area: 131,460 sq. mi.
Population: 2,441,000
Capital: Brazzaville
(586,000)
Official language: French
Currency: Franc CFA
Main exports: Petroleum,
timber, coffee, cocoa

Cameroon

Equatorial
Guinea

São Tomé and
Príncipe

Gabon

Congo

Geography

The coast of West Africa is fringed with mangroves and mudflats washed with warm rain blown in from the ocean. Inland, lagoons and coastal swamps give way to lush tropical rain forests that stretch hundreds of kilometers. Meandering rivers often provide the only form of transportation, as the jungle encroaches on mud-built roads that get washed away in the rainy season. The steaming forests rise to cooler central highlands. Rivers here sometimes tumble from spectacular heights into deep gorges. During the rains they flood the land with fertile mud, occasionally washing away whole settlements of houses. Finally the landscape opens out into an interior of savanna grasslands that shimmer in the heat.

Togo dancers
• • • • • • • • • • • • • • • • •

In Togo, traditional dancers wear horns, scarves, and brightly colored beaded kilts as they prepare for a ritual celebration.

Central and East Africa

Zaire is crossed by the great Zaire River (Congo), which forms the country's chief means of transportation. In the north, the humid, thundery climate supports a vast area of dense rain forest. To the south are open savannas. Large areas of land have been set aside by the Zairean government as wildlife sanctuaries.

The raging river torrents that cross Zaire offer massive hydroelectric potential, while the rocks conceal deposits of uranium and gold. Zaire is a world leader in the production of copper, cobalt, and industrial diamonds, but most Zaireans are subsistence farmers. In 1996 tragedy struck twice for Zaire. The world price of copper fell, causing poverty and hardship, and war broke out with Rwanda.

Uganda

Uganda's rich red farmland and equatorial climate support coffee, bananas, corn, and millet. Uganda also has thick green forest, arid scrubland and beautiful lakes.

During the 1970s Uganda was ruled by General Idi Amin. Ugandan Asians were expelled, businesses collapsed, and Amin's political opponents were murdered. Amin was overthrown in 1979. Ugandan governments since then have worked to unite the country and repair its economy.

Central African Republic

Central African Republic has high grassy plains and lush rain forest. In the rainy season roads become a sea of mud, so rivers are used for transport. Diamonds are mined and other exports are rubber, cotton, and timber. Trade is mainly with France, which

CABINDA
(Angola)

Kins
Matadi

Masai women

Masai women wear bright cloth and beaded collars for a ceremony in which their sons will become junior elders.

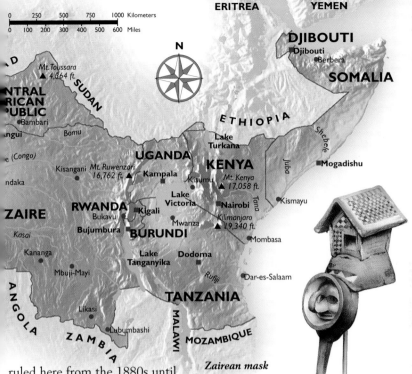

ruled here from the 1880s until independence in 1960. For 14 years the country was ruled by Jean-Bedel Bokassa, a despot who declared himself its emperor and lived in luxury while ordinary people went hungry. In 1993 he was removed from power and the people chose a new leader in democratic elections.

Zairean mask
. . . .
This carved mask is held over the face by Yaka boys during ceremonies to mark their passage into manhood. The Yaka people live in southern Zaire.

Mogadishu
. . . .
These whitewashed buildings in Somalia's capital city and chief port are designed in the Arab style.

Djibouti   **Somalia**   **Kenya**   **Tanzania**   **Uganda**

■ **DJIBOUTI**
Area: 8,920 sq. mi.
Population: 481,000
Capital: Djibouti
(317,000)
Official languages:
Arabic, French
Currency: Djibouti franc
Main exports: Hides,
livestock, coffee in
transit from Ethiopia

■ **SOMALIA**
Area: 283,560 sq. mi.
Population: 9,517,000
Capital: Mogadishu
(1,000,000)
Official languages:
Somali, Arabic
Currency: Somali shilling
Main exports: Bananas,
livestock, hides

■ **KENYA**
Area: 223,970 sq. mi.
Population: 28,113,000
Capital: Nairobi
(1,104,000)
Official languages:
Swahili, English
Currency: Kenya shilling
Main exports: Tea, coffee,
fruit, petroleum products

■ **TANZANIA**
Area: 363,270 sq. mi.
Population: 28,783,000
Capital: Dodoma
(204,000)
Official languages:
Swahili, English
Currency: Tanzanian
shilling
Main exports: Coffee,
cotton, sisal, cloves,
tobacco

■ **UGANDA**
Area: 92,650 sq. mi.
Population: 19,246,000
Capital: Kampala
(774,000)
Official language:
English
Currency: Uganda shilling
Main exports: Coffee,
cotton, tea, tobacco

■ **RWANDA**
Area: 10,120 sq. mi.
Population: 7,789,000
Capital: Kigali (157,000)
Official languages:
Kinyarwanda, French
Currency: Rwanda franc
Main exports: Coffee,
tea, tin

■ **BURUNDI**
Area: 10,700 sq. mi.
Population: 5,985,000
Capital: Bujumbura
(236,000)
Official languages:
Kirundi, French
Currency: Burundi franc
Main exports: Coffee, tea,
bananas

■ **ZAIRE**
Area: 901,370 sq. mi.
Population: 41,166,000
Capital: Kinshasa
(3,804,000)
Official language: French
Currency: Zaire
Main exports: Copper,
coffee, diamonds, cobalt,
petroleum

■ **CENTRAL AFRICAN
REPUBLIC**
Area: 239,270 sq. mi.
Population: 3,258,000
Capital: Bangui
(452,000)
Official language: French
Currency: Franc CFA
Main exports: Coffee,
diamonds, timber,
cotton, tobacco

Rwanda   **Burundi**   **Zaire**   **Central African
Republic**

Mandrill
● ●

*Mandrills are large monkeys related to
baboons. They are powerful animals with
colorful faces and buttocks that live in
small family groups in the rain forests of
central West Africa. They climb trees to
pick fruit and dig for roots and insects.*

Rwanda and Burundi

The villages of Rwanda and Burundi cling to green, tropical hillsides. These countries have river valleys, grassland, volcanoes, and swamps. Most people are farmers who herd goats and cattle and grow bananas, beans, corn, and cassava. The majority belong to a group of people called the Hutu, but a minority are Tutsis.

For hundreds of years the Tutsis held power while the Hutus were poor peasant farmers. In the late 1890s Ruanda-Urundi (the two countries combined) became first a German, then a Belgian colony. After independence in 1962 Hutus gained power in Rwanda and years of violence against the Tutsis followed. Many fled to Burundi where Tutsis remained in control, suppressing Hutu uprisings. In 1994 the leaders of Rwanda and Burundi were killed in a plane crash, believed to have been caused by terrorists. A bitter war between Hutus and Tutsis broke out in both countries. Millions of innocent people were killed and others fled as refugees to Tanzania and Zaire. A major international relief effort was instigated to help both nations. In 1996 war broke out again between the Hutus and Tutsis of Rwanda and Zaire.

Tutsi dancers

∙ ∙ ∙ ∙ ∙ ∙ ∙ ∙ ∙ ∙ ∙ ∙ ∙ ∙ ∙ ∙ ∙ ∙ ∙ ∙

Tutsi men wearing plumed headdresses perform a ceremonial lion dance. Tutsis live in Rwanda, Burundi, and Zaire.

Tanzanian stew

∙ ∙ ∙ ∙ ∙ ∙ ∙ ∙ ∙ ∙ ∙ ∙ ∙ ∙ ∙ ∙

Tanzanian beef stew is made with coconut milk, tomatoes, and plantains. Plantain is like banana, but needs to be cooked.

Taxis in Kampala, Uganda

∙ ∙

Vans park in the market district of Kampala, Uganda's capital. They operate as shared taxis. Now roads have been repaired after long years of war, they offer a better service than the railroads.

151

Kenya

Kenya is one of the most beautiful countries in Africa. The low coastal plain with its thick tropical forests rises to a broad grassland plateau. In the north is a parched desert and to the west are the ancient volcanoes and craggy cliffs of the Great Rift Valley. Tourists are attracted by the wildlife, the scenery, white beaches, and luxury hotels, but few see the other side of Kenya. There is poor housing on the edge of Nairobi and laborers on coffee plantations and commercial farms are badly paid. Educational standards are high, but many people cannot find jobs. Unemployment increased when large numbers of refugees flooded in to escape the civil war in neighboring Somalia.

Tanzanian carver
. . . .

A Makonde carver works on a wooden sculpture. The Makonde people, who live on the coast and the Mozambique border are renowned for their skill at carving.

Tanzania

The snow-covered mass of Mount Kilimanjaro—Africa's highest mountain—looms high above northern Tanzania, close to the border with Kenya. To the west of Kilimanjaro are other natural wonders such as the Ngorongoro Crater, the center of an ancient volcano inhabited only by elephants, rhinoceroses, hyenas, and other wild animals. Vast herds of zebras, antelopes, wildebeests, and the lions and cheetahs that prey on them roam the Serengeti Plains. Clouds of dust mark the passing of cattle and their Masai herders. The climate is cooler in the mountainous areas in the north and south of the country. The south also has the huge Selous Wildlife Reserve, one of the largest wildlife reserves in the world.

Tanzania's economy is based on agriculture, although two thirds of the country cannot be farmed because of lack of water and swarms of disease-carrying tsetse flies. The coastal region is fertile, producing bananas, mangoes, sugarcane, and sisal. Other important crops are tea, coffee, tobacco, and cotton.

Kenyan bottle
. . . .

This beautifully decorated bottle has been made by a Kikuyu craftsman out of a gourd, a plant like a squash. Kenyans are famed for their artistic skill.

152

Somalia

Somalia is a hot, dry country. Most Somalis are nomads who live by herding camels, sheep, and goats. In the south farmers grow crops such as bananas, citrus fruits, and sugarcane.

The north of the country was ruled by the British from 1884 and Italy controlled the south from 1905. These colonies were important because their ports lay on international shipping routes. They joined to become one independent nation in 1960.

Somalia is a poor country and it suffered from severe drought in the 1970s and 1980s. The nomads faced starvation when their herds died and in 1974 war broke out with Ethiopia. Somalia agreed a peace treaty with Ethiopia in 1988. But in the 1990s civil war between Somali clans led to thousands of deaths.

Well in Somalia
• • • • • • • • • • • • • • • • • • •

Children draw water from a well in Bardera, Somalia. Drinking water is vital to their survival, as Somalians have less to eat than any other people in the world.

Djibouti

Djibouti is mainly a wilderness of scrub and rock. The economy is dependent on shipping and the country is named for its capital city, a major port situated on important trade routes between the Gulf of Aden and the Red Sea. Djibouti has been the chief port for trade with Ethiopia since it was built by French colonists in the 1800s.

In the past most of Djibouti's people—two groups called the Afars and the Issas—were nomads, herding sheep, goats, camels, and cattle in the deserts and mountains. Many still live in this way, but increasing numbers leave the countryside to seek work in the port. Some go even farther, finding jobs in countries such as Saudi Arabia.

Somali bread
• • • • • • • • • • • • • • • • • • •

A Somali woman pours dough on to a griddle to make anjeera. *This flat, unleavened bread is shaped like a pancake and eaten with stew.*

153

Southern Africa

At the heart of this land is a high flat plateau of vast plains and bush. This is the savanna grassland. Parts of it have been turned into reserves for the protection of wild animals. This region is tropical, but the high altitude gives it a mild climate. In the west, much of Angola and Namibia is a sandy wasteland. The Namib Desert is one of the driest places on Earth. The Kalahari Desert spreads east into Botswana. At the tip of the continent is South Africa, a land of great scenic beauty dominated by the dramatic Drakensberg Mountains. In the east it is hot and humid, with tropical rain forest covering the lower land near the coast. The great rivers of southern Africa, including the Orange and the mightly Zambezi, are dammed to provide hydroelectric power and water for irrigation.

CABINDA
(Angola)

CONGO

ZAIRE

TANZANIA

Ruvuma

Luanda

Cuanza

Lobito

Huambo

ANGOLA

Lubango

Namibe

Cunene

Cubango

Cuito

Cuando

Lake Benguela

Ndola

ZAMBIA

Lusaka

Zambezi

Lake Kariba

MALAWI

Lilongwe

Lake Nyasa (Malawi)

Moçan

MOZAMBIQ

Harare

ZIMBABWE

Zambezi

Okavango Swamp

NAMIBIA

Windhoek

Francistown

Bulawayo

Beira

Walvis Bay

Kalahari Desert

BOTSWANA

Save

Limpopo

Mozambique Channel

Gaborone

Namib Desert

Lüderitz

Pretoria

Johannesburg

Mbabane

Maputo

Vaal

Kimberley

Bloemfontein

SWAZILAND

Orange

Maseru

LESOTHO

Durban

To

INDIAN OCEAN

SOUTH AFRICA

Drakensberg

East London

Cape Town

Port Elizabeth

ATLANTIC OCEAN

0 250 500 750 1000 Kilometers
0 100 200 300 400 500 Miles

N

154

History

In the 1800s diamonds and gold were discovered here and fortune hunters began to rush in from Europe. The countries of Southern Africa were seized by Portugal, Germany, Britain, Netherlands, and France. Hungry for wealth, the Europeans conquered the African tribes, or tricked them into selling mining rights. Thus the enormous riches yielded up by the land benefited only the white minority.

In 1950 the white government of South Africa, the continent's richest country, introduced the policy of apartheid. This separated blacks from whites and refused them equal rights. The cruel regime left millions in grinding poverty. In 1994 democratic elections gave South Africa its first majority black government led by

South Africa's parliament
. . . .

For more than a century, only whites were allowed inside South Africa's parliament. In 1994 South Africa became a multiracial democracy.

President Nelson Mandela. His triumph brought hope to all the peoples of southern Africa, where the colonial past has left many with poor housing, inadequate education, and limited job opportunities.

MOROS

Antseranana

Mahajanga

Toamasina

Antananarivo

ADAGASCAR

Fianarantsoa

Ringtail lemur
. . . .

This rare lemur is found only on Madagascar. It evolved when the island split from the mainland 160 million years ago.

Delicious honeycomb
. . . .

A San man from Botswana enjoys a honeycomb. To get the honeycomb, the San climb a tree and smoke out the bees. The bee grubs in the comb are considered the tastiest delicacy.

Angola

Namibia

South Africa

Swaziland

Zimbabwe

■ ANGOLA
Area: 1,479,230 sq. mi.
Population: 10,276,000
Capital: Luanda
(1,200,000)
Official language:
Portuguese
Currency: Kwanza
Main exports: Crude oil,
coffee, diamonds, fish
products, sisal, corn,
palm oil

■ LESOTHO
Area: 11,670 sq. mi.
Population: 1,882,000
Capital: Maseru
(110,000)
Official language:
Sesotho, English
Currency: Loti
Main exports: Wool,
mohair, diamonds,
wheat, vegetables,
livestock

■ MOZAMBIQUE
Area: 307,280 sq. mi.
Population: 15,322,000
Capital: Maputo
(1,098,000)
Official language:
Portuguese
Currency: Metical
Main exports: Shrimp,
cashew nuts, sugar,
petroleum products,
copra, cotton

■ BOTSWANA
Area: 223,620 sq. mi.
Population: 1,143,000
Capital: Gaborone
(139,000)
Official language: English
Currency: Pula
Main exports: Diamonds,
copper, nickel, meat and
meat products, hides,
textiles

■ SOUTH AFRICA
Area: 1,433,220 sq. mi.
Population: 40,774,000
Capitals: Cape Town
(2,351,000), Pretoria,
Bloemfontein
Official languages: 11,
including English,
Ndebele, Afrikaans
Currency: Rand
Main exports: Gold,
metals, diamonds, food
products, machinery

■ SWAZILAND
Area: 6,670 sq. mi.
Population: 814,000
Capital: Mbabane
(39,000)
Official languages:
English, Siswati
Currency: Lilangeni
Main exports: Sugar,
wood and forest
products, canned fruit,
citrus fruit, asbestos

■ MADAGASCAR
Area: 225,660 sq. mi.
Population: 13,259,000
Capital: Antananarivo
(804,000)
Official languages:
Malagasy, French
Currency: Malagasy franc
Main exports: Coffee,
cloves, vanilla, sugar,
sisal, shrimp

■ MALAWI
Area: 45,540 sq. mi.
Population: 9,135,000
Capital: Lilongwe
(234,000)
Official languages:
Chichewa, English
Currency: Kwacha
Main exports: Tobacco,
sugar, tea, cotton,
peanuts

■ SEYCHELLES
Area: 175 sq. mi.
Population: 72,000
Capital: Victoria (25,000)
Official languages:
Creole, English, French
Currency: Seychelles
rupee
Main exports: Copra,
fish, cinnamon

■ MAURITIUS
Area: 784 sq. mi.
Population: 1,098,000
Capital: Port Louis
(144,000)
Official language: English
Currency: Mauritius
rupee
Main exports: Sugar,
clothing, tea, toys, games

Zambia

Malawi

Mozambique

Madagascar

Seychelles

Lesotho

Botswana

■ ZAMBIA
Area: 289,300 sq. mi.
Population: 8,885,000
Capital: Lusaka
(921,000)
Official language: English
Currency: Kwacha
Main exports: Copper,
cobalt, zinc, emeralds,
lead, tobacco

■ ZIMBABWE
Area: 150,140 sq. mi.
Population: 10,898,000
Capital: Harare
(657,000)
Official language: English
Currency: Zimbabwe
dollar
Main exports: Tobacco,
iron alloys, gold, nickel,
cotton, steel

■ NAMIBIA
Area: 316,850 sq. mi.
Population: 1,584,000
Capital: Windhoek
(125,000)
Official language: English
Currency: Namibian
dollar
Main exports: Diamonds,
uranium, fish products,
meat products, livestock

■ COMOROS
Area: 1,715 sq. mi.
Population: 607,000
Capital: Moroni (22,000)
Official languages:
French, Arabic
Currency: Comorian franc
Main exports: Vanilla,
cloves, ylang ylang,
copra, coffee

Comoros

Mauritius

Economy

Mining has always formed the backbone of the economy in southern Africa. The oldest known mines in the world are in Swaziland, where iron ore was mined 43,000 years ago. Diamonds are found in large quantities in the volcanic rocks of South Africa, which exports more of these precious gems than any other country on Earth. South Africa also has the world's biggest goldfield and considerable reserves of coal. Zambia's main export is copper, found near the border with Zaire. Mines in the Namib Desert produce uranium, a highly radioactive metal used in nuclear power stations.

Cattle are reared on the grassy plains of South Africa, which also produces large quanitites of grapes and grain. Tropical fruits grow in the lush eastern lands. But arid conditions make farming difficult in much of this region.

Mauritian children
• • • • • • • • • • • •

A group of children from a fishing community show the mix of different peoples who live in Mauritius. They are the descendants of European settlers, Chinese and Indian traders, and African slaves.

Fruits of Zimbabwe
• • • • • • • • • • • •

Mango, passion fruit, pineapple, and avocado are four of the delicious fruits cultivated in Zimbabwe.

AUSTRALASIA

The isolated position of this continent, which includes Australia, New Zealand, and the Pacific Islands, means that the wildlife found here is often very different from that in the rest of the world. The only two mammals in the world that lay eggs, the duck-billed platypus and the echidna (a spiny anteater), are found in Australia and New Guinea. These countries are also the home of pouched mammals called marsupials, which include kangaroos, wallabies, koala bears, and wombats.

Maori woodcarving

The Maoris came to New Zealand around AD800. They crossed the Pacific in wooden boats and developed the art of woodcarving with distinctive figures of gods and demons.

Australia's landscapes include desert, rain forest, eucalyptus woodland, muddy creeks, and scrub. The climate changes from tropical in the north to temperate in the south. Low plateaus and plains, dotted with large expanses of scrub and desert, take up much of the land. New Zealand, which is made up of two main islands, is a mountainous country with hot springs and geysers in the north and glaciers in the south. Coconut groves and rain forests thrive on the Pacific Islands. Turtles, crabs, and seabirds from the Pacific Ocean visit the islands' coral reefs and sandy shores.

■ **CONTINENTAL FACTS**
Area: 3,271,240 sq. mi. (95% of this is Australia and New Zealand)
Population: 28,000,000
Independent countries: 14
Largest country: Australia
Smallest country: Nauru
Highest point: Mt. Wilhelm (15,396 ft.) in Papua New Guinea
Lowest point: Lake Eyre (39 ft. below sea level) in Australia
Longest rivers: Murray (1,596 mi.) and its tributary, the Darling (1,699 mi.), in Australia

Didgeridoo

Aboriginals today still play the didgeridoo, a traditional pipe made of tree branches that sounds very deep notes. The instrument is so long it has to be rested on the ground.

Polynesian harvest

Fruits and vegetables were taken from their east Asian homelands by the early Polynesian settlers on their voyages over the Pacific. Today these are important crops in the Polynesian islands.

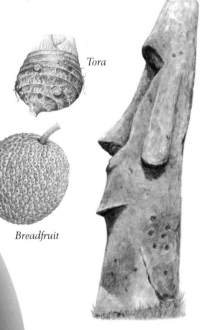

Coconut

Yam

Tora

Breadfruit

Easter Island

About 600 strange stone heads were left behind on Easter Island by early Polynesian settlers. This island is owned by Chile, though it lies nearly 2,500 miles off its western shores. The sculptures are around 1,000 years old.

The Pacific Islands

Most of the Pacific Islands were formed by fierce volcanic activity, which continues today. Some islands, such as New Caledonia and the main islands of the Fiji, Samoa, and Vanuatu groups, have steep, forested mountains. Others are low islands formed from corals, the tiny warm-water creatures that live inside chalky skeletons. Volcanoes that have collapsed into the water may be capped by a ring of coral growth called an atoll. This is made from coral remains that have built up around underwater mountains and ridges until they stick out above the sea. Both mountainous and low islands are often surrounded by coral reefs.

The Pacific Islands are coping with rapid political and economic changes. The Melanesians, Micronesians, and Polynesians have recently founded independent states, although some islands and island groups remain overseas territories of France, the U.S.A., Australia, or New Zealand. Many of the smaller islands have had to rely on economic aid from larger countries to help them develop. Years of colonial rule brought mining and the testing of nuclear weapons to some islands, causing serious environmental damage. Today tourism and industry create some wealth, but often

WAKE ISLAND (U.S.A.)

NORTHERN MARIANA ISLANDS (U.S.A.)

GUAM (U.S.A.)

PALAU

FEDERATED STA OF MICRONES

NAURU

IRIAN JAYA (INDONESIA)

PAPUA NEW GUINEA

SOLOMON ISLANDS

TU

Arafura Sea

Port Moresby

VANU

Coral Sea

AUSTRALIA

NEW CALEDONIA (Fr.)

Tasman Sea

NEW ZEALAND

Queen Alexandra's birdwing

The Queen Alexandra's birdwing is the largest butterfly in the world, with a wingspan of up to 11 in. It is found in the tropical forests of Papua New Guinea.

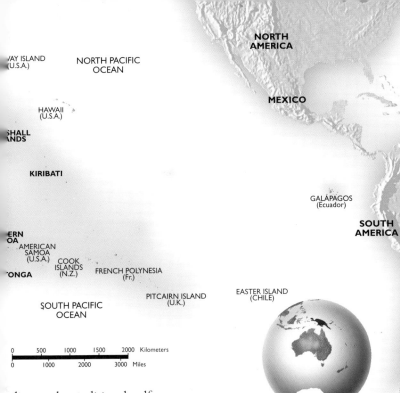

NORTH
AMERICA

NORTH PACIFIC
OCEAN

WAY ISLAND
(U.S.A.)

MEXICO

HAWAII
(U.S.A.)

SHALL
NDS

KIRIBATI

GALÁPAGOS
(Ecuador)

SOUTH
AMERICA

ERN
OA

AMERICAN
SAMOA
(U.S.A.)

COOK
ISLANDS
(N.Z.)

FRENCH POLYNESIA
(Fr.)

ONGA

SOUTH PACIFIC
OCEAN

PITCAIRN ISLAND
(U.K.)

EASTER ISLAND
(CHILE)

| 0 | 500 | 1000 | 1500 | 2000 | Kilometers |
| 0 | | 1000 | 2000 | 3000 | Miles |

disrupt the traditional, self-sufficient way of life based on fishing and farming. However, modern communications have also helped to bring together remote communities of islanders.

Unu bona boroma

This dish from Papua New Guinea consists of breadfruit, bacon, and onions. Breadfruit is a vegetable grown throughout the South Pacific.

Polynesian sculptor

A sculptor carves a stone tiki (mythical figure) on an island in French Polynesia. Islanders also practice wood carving and mat weaving.

161

Papua New Guinea

The country of Papua New Guinea lies on the eastern half of New Guinea, the second largest island in the world. The western half of the island is part of Indonesia. Papua New Guinea also includes many small islands, such as the Bismarck Archipelago and the northern Solomon Islands. In the 1800s European traders and missionaries settled here. Germany and Britain controlled different parts of Papua New Guinea until 1920 when Australia took over. Independence finally came to the country in 1975.

Papua New Guinea is a land of mountains, fast-flowing rivers, and dense forests. Its fertile soils support vast plantations of coconuts, coffee, tea, palm oil, and rubber. Grassy lowlands and marshes are home to tortoises and crocodiles. Other wildlife includes giant butterflies, large flightless

birds called cassowaries, and marsupials such as possums.

Most people live in rural areas, often in remote valleys that are inaccessible by road. This has meant that a huge variety of customs and languages has developed—more than 700 languages are spoken. Traditional ways of life are still strong, with communities growing their own food and hunting animals.

Kiribati
• •

A Kiribati islander weaves a mat from strips of dried palm leaf. Coconut palms also provide fresh coconut and copra (dried coconut) for export and leaves for roofing.

American Samoa
• •

Tuna are offloaded at the dock at Pago Pago in American Samoa. Fishing is a major industry here, with large catches canned for export.

162

Fijian atoll
• •

This aerial view of a Fijian atoll shows clearly how an underwater mountain of coral built up over the years until its peak rose above the surface of the sea and formed an island.

Fishing in the South Pacific
• •

Traditionally, islanders fish at night. They set fire to palm branches and hang them over the side of the boat. The fish swim toward the light and are speared or shot with arrows by the islanders.

Nauru

Nauru is one of the world's smallest independent countries. Most of its people live on the coast. Almost all the rest of the island consists of a plateau that once contained large deposits of phosphate rock. The phosphate was created by seabirds living on the island. Over millions of years their droppings built up to form phosphate rock. Phosphate, a valuable source of fertilizer, is Nauru's only export.

The people of Nauru used to grow their own food and farm fish in the shallow lagoons. However, 100 years of phosphate mining has reduced much of the island to desert and nearly all the island's food has to be imported. Today the government is trying to develop other industries and restore over-mined land so that it can be used for growing the island's own food again.

The Marshall Islands

These islands are named for the British sea captain John Marshall, who landed here in the late 1700s. The group consists of 31 islands and atolls. Their resources include phosphate, which is used to make fertilizers, and beautiful beaches that attract tourists. The islanders grow papaya, breadfruit, and arrowroot (a starchy root).

Like other Pacific islands, the Marshall Islands have been ruled by various foreign powers. They were colonized by Germany in the 1880s, then ruled by Japan and the United States. Independence finally came in 1991.

163

Tuvalu

Tuvalu is made up of nine low-lying islands that form coral atolls around peaceful blue lagoons. Eight of Tuvalu's islands are inhabited. They have the highest population density in the Pacific, along with Nauru.

The islands' soil is very poor and there are few natural resources. Islanders grow bananas and taro (a starchy root) to eat and keep chickens and pigs. Fishing is also important. Coconut palms grow everywhere and copra (dried coconut kernels) is exported along with handicrafts such as woven mats and baskets. Many young islanders try to find jobs on ocean ships to earn money. Another growing source of income is charging foreign ships money to fish for tuna around the island chain. The sale of Tuvalu postage stamps to dealers also raises some income.

Micronesia
• •

This aerial view shows some of the 600 islands that make up the Federated States of Micronesia. Rainfall here is high and the islands are subject to typhoons that often reach speeds of 150 mph.

■ NEW CALEDONIA
Area: 7,140 sq. mi.
Population: 179,000
Capital: Nouméa (66,000)
Official language: French
Currency: Franc CFP
Main exports: Nickel, copra

■ FEDERATED STATES OF MICRONESIA
Area: 270 sq. mi.
Population: 114,000
Capital: Palikir, on Pohnpei (7,000)
Official language: English
Currency: US dollar
Main export: Copra

■ PALAU
Area: 188 sq. mi.
Population: 16,000
Capital: Koror (10,000)
Official languages: Palauan, English
Currency: US dollar
Main exports: Copra, tuna

■ THE MARSHALL ISLANDS
Area: 69 sq. mi.
Population: 52,000
Capital: Majuro (20,000)
Official languages: Marshallese, English
Currency: US dollar
Main export: Copra

■ KIRIBATI
Area: 280 sq. mi.
Population: 75,000
Capital: Bairiki, on Tarawa (25,000)
Official language: English
Currency: Australian dollar
Main exports: Copra, fish

Papua New Guinea

Palau

Solomon Islands

French Polynesia

■ NAURU
Area: 7.6 sq. mi.
Population: 10,000
Seat of government: Yaren
Official language: Nauruan
Currency: Australian dollar
Main export: Phosphate

■ SOLOMON ISLANDS
Area: 10,900 sq. mi.
Population: 354,000
Capital: Honiara (34,000)
Official language: English
Currency: Solomon Islands dollar
Main exports: Fish products, timber, copra, cocoa beans, palm oil products

■ TUVALU
Area: 9.2 sq. mi.
Population: 13,000
Capital: Fongafale, on Funafuti Atoll (3,000)
Official languages: Tuvaluan, English
Currency: Australian dollar
Main export: Copra

■ FRENCH POLYNESIA
Area: 1,260 sq. mi.
Population: 212,000
Capital: Papeete, on Tahiti (79,000)
Official languages: French, Tahitian
Currency: Franc CFP
Main exports: Coconut oil, cultured pearls

■ FIJI
Area: 7,050 sq. mi.
Population: 747,000
Capital: Suva (72,000)
Official language: English
Currency: Fiji dollar
Main exports: Sugar, gold, fish, clothes

■ WESTERN SAMOA
Area: 1,090 sq. mi.
Population: 158,000
Capital: Apia (33,000)
Official languages: Samoan, English
Currency: Tala
Main exports: Taro, coconut

■ AMERICAN SAMOA
Area: 77 sq. mi.
Population: 38,000
Capital: Pago Pago
Official languages: Samoan, English
Currency: US dollar
Main exports: Tuna, copra

■ VANUATU
Area: 4,690 sq. mi.
Population: 156,000
Capital: Port-Vila (20,000)
Official languages: Bislama, English, French
Currency: Vatu
Main exports: Copra, beef, timber

■ TONGA
Area: 288 sq. mi.
Population: 98,000
Capital: Nukualofa (29,000)
Official languages: Tongan, English
Currency: Pa'anga
Main exports: Coconut products, copra, vanilla

■ PAPUA NEW GUINEA
Area: 17,790 sq. mi.
Population: 3,922,000
Capital: Port Moresby (194,000)
Official language: English
Currency: Kina
Main exports: Gold coffee, copper, timber, cocoa, copra products

Federated States of Micronesia

Marshall Islands

Kiribati

Tuvalu

Nauru

Fiji

Western Samoa

American Samoa

Vanuatu

Tonga

New Zealand

New Zealand is made up of two large islands, North Island and South Island, and a number of smaller islands, some far off in the South Pacific. This spectacular land has towering mountain ranges, lush forests, rolling grasslands, and long sandy beaches. On North Island there are several active volcanoes and many hot springs and geysers. Unique species of birds, reptiles, and plants have developed in New Zealand, cut off from the rest of the world by hundreds of miles of sea.

It is believed that the country was first settled by a people called the Maoris during the AD800s. Europeans first visited New Zealand in 1642 and started to settle in the late 1700s. Between 1840 and 1907 this country was a British colony and today most of its people are of British descent. New Zealand is now an independent country with a high

- **NEW ZEALAND**
  Area: 103,990 sq. mi.
  Population: 3,520,000
  Capital: Wellington (326,000)
  Official language: English
  Currency: New Zealand dollar
  Main exports: Meat, milk, butter, cheese, wool, fish, fruit

standard of living and a strong tradition of equality. In 1893 it became the first country in the world to give women the vote.

A temperate climate and plentiful rainfall make New Zealand a good farming country. Although there is some industry, the economy is largely dependent on agriculture. The meat, wool, and dairy products from sheep and cattle raised on New Zealand's green pastures are exported all over the world. New Zealand's native evergreen forests are mostly protected, but extensive plantations of conifer and eucalyptus trees supply sawmills and the pulp and paper industry.

Baked kumaras
. . . .

Kumaras (sweet potatoes) are a traditional Maori food. They are often baked and served with pork and apple or with lamb.

Hydroelectric dam
. . . .

This dam at Roxburgh on the Clutha River powers one of New Zealand's 30 hydroelectric schemes, which provide 75% of the country's electricity.

North Cape

0 50 100 150 200 250 Kilometers
0 50 100 150 Miles

N

• Whangarei

• Auckland

Hamilton •

Waikato

• Rotorua

Lake Taupo

Gisborne •

New Plymouth •

Mt. Ruapehu ▲ 9,175 ft.

Mt. Egmont ▲ 8,260 ft.

NORTH ISLAND

Napier •

Hastings •

NEW ZEALAND

Wanganui •

Palmerston North •

■ **WELLINGTON**

Nelson •

Blenheim •

SOUTH PACIFIC OCEAN

Greymouth •

Tasman Sea

Southern Alps

Mt. Cook ▲ 12,349 ft.

Rakaia

• Christchurch

SOUTH ISLAND • Timaru

Waitaki

...ord ...nd

Lake Te Anau

Clutha

• Dunedin

Invercargill •

STEWART ISLAND

Whakarewarewa
• • • • • • • • • • • • • • • •

Clouds of steam shoot into the air from volcanic rock at Whakarewarewa, near Rotorua on North Island. New Zealand has many geysers and hot springs. They are the result of high temperatures deep inside the earth.

Weta
• • • • • • • • • • • • • • • •

The weta is a flightless insect that looks like a large grasshopper. The weta grows to about 4 in. long and is found on Pacific islands offshore of New Zealand.

167

Geography

North Island has an irregular coastline fringed by inlets and sandy beaches with peninsulas projecting into the sea. Fertile lowlands rise inland to hills. The center of North Island is a volcanic region. Four volcanoes are still active and there are many hot bubbling springs and geysers. Earthquakes are common, but rarely severe. Farther south, rugged hills descend to plains and coastal lowlands.

South Island, just 16 miles away across the Cook Strait, is dominated by the soaring peaks of the Southern Alps with their snowfields and glaciers. Many beautiful lakes lying in thickly forested mountain valleys feed fast-flowing rivers. To the east of the Alps lie the fertile Canterbury Plains, New Zealand's largest area of flat land. In the far southwest spectacular fjords cut narrow gashes into the land.

New Zealand is home to many unique plants, such as the scarlet-flowered pohutukawa. The native forests are mainly made up of evergreen trees and ferns. Since 1900 many new tree species have been introduced into New Zealand. The country's paper industry depends on the radiata pine, originally imported from California.

Most of New Zealand's animals have been introduced from other parts of the world. Deer, cattle, and rabbits were brought by European settlers. Wallabies and brush-tailed possums came from Australia.

The kiwi, a large bird that cannot fly, is the country's national animal. Many wildlife habitats throughout the islands are now national parks.

Economy

New Zealand is a land of farms. For every person who lives here, there are about 20 farm animals. Sheep produce the country's world-famous lamb and wool. Large herds of cattle are raised for New Zealand's other major exports, beef, milk, cheese, and butter. Crops include wheat, corn, barley, and apples. Vineyards produce high-quality wines.

Food processing is the country's main industry. Textiles, aluminum, and plastics are also manufactured. New Zealand harnesses the power of its swift-flowing rivers to produce hydroelectricity. There are also reserves of oil, natural gas, coal, and gold. But tourism has recently outstripped all the country's other ways of earning money.

The old Parliament Building with its new Executive Wing stands at the heart of Wellington, New Zealand's capital city in North Island. Wellington was founded by British settlers in 1840.

People and history

The majority of New Zealanders are descended from European settlers, mostly British, although more than 10 percent are Maori people. The Maoris originally came from the eastern Pacific. A large part of the population is also of mixed Maori and European descent.

The first European to discover the islands was the Dutch navigator, Abel Tasman, in 1642. British settlers founded Wellington, on North Island, in 1840 and New Zealand became a British colony. After gold was discovered on

South Island in 1861 a rush of settlers arrived to try and make their fortunes. During the 1860s the settlers and the Maoris quarreled over land and a number of fierce wars occurred. As a result, the Maoris lost many of their ancestral lands and rights.

New Zealand became an independent nation in 1907, but kept its strong political and economic links with Britain. More recently the country has developed closer ties with Australia and other Pacific nations. Following a period of Maori unrest in the 1970s, there is now a new interest in Maori culture and traditions.

Tuatara
* * * * * * * * *

Unique to New Zealand, the tuatara is the sole survivor of a group of lizards that lived on Earth millions of years ago.

Kiwi
* *

The kiwi leaves its burrow by night to probe for grubs and worms with its long sensitive bill, which is fringed with bristles. Although it is a bird it cannot fly. Strict laws protect the kiwi from extinction.

Australia

■ **AUSTRALIA**
Area: 2,965,017 sq. mi.
Population: 17,684,000
Capital: Canberra (279,000)
Official language: English
Currency: Australian dollar
Main exports: Gold, other metals and metal ores, diamonds, coal, meat, wool, cereals

Australia is a vast country with a relatively small population. Most Australians live on a narrow strip of land extending along the east and southeast coasts. The interior, known as the outback, is too dry and barren to support many people. Much of it is desert or scrubby grassland where it may not rain for years at a time. However, rich deposits of minerals and grazing for vast numbers of cattle and sheep make the outback a major source of wealth for the country.

The first inhabitants of Australia were the Aboriginal peoples, who originally came from Southeast Asia about 40,000 years ago. During the 1700s Australia became a British colony and thousands of people who had committed crimes in Britain were given the choice of either going to prison or moving to Australia. As a result many Australians are of British descent and the country has maintained strong links with the U.K. The head of the state is still the British monarch, but in recent years a movement to make the country a republic has gathered strength.

Funnel-web spider

As its name suggests, the funnel-web spider spins a funnel-shaped web. The bite of some funnel-webs can be fatal to humans.

Broo

Ashburton

Carnarvon

**WESTE
AUSTRA**

Murchison

● Geraldton

Kalgc

★ **Perth**
● Fremantle

Parliament House

Australia's Parliament House in Canberra was built in 1988. Australia is a federation of six states and two territories. It has a federal government that decides national issues, and separate state governments.

Three Sisters Rock

The Three Sisters is an unusual rock formation at Katoomba near Sydney in New South Wales. The rock has been eroded to leave three pinnacles.

Lamingtons

Lamingtons are an afternoon treat in Australia. They are squares of sponge cake covered in chocolate and coconut. Most Australian recipes originate in Europe.

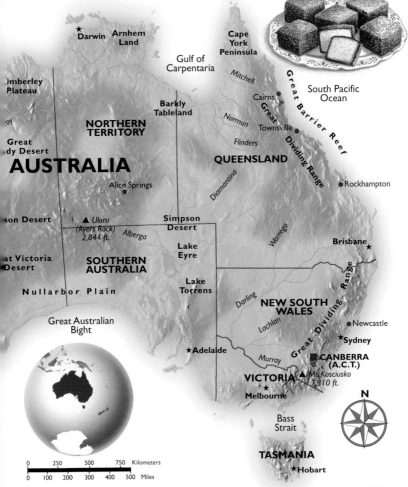

Darwin
Arnhem Land

imberley Plateau

oy

Great dy Desert

AUSTRALIA

NORTHERN TERRITORY

Alice Springs

son Desert

▲ Uluru (Ayers Rock) 2,844 ft.

at Victoria Desert

SOUTHERN AUSTRALIA

Nullarbor Plain

Great Australian Bight

Cape York Peninsula

Gulf of Carpentaria

Mitchell

Cairns

Norman

Townsville

Flinders

Great Barrier Reef

South Pacific Ocean

Barkly Tableland

QUEENSLAND

Diamantina

Great Dividing Range

● Rockhampton

Simpson Desert

Alberga

Lake Eyre

Lake Torrens

Warrego

Brisbane ★

Darling

NEW SOUTH WALES

Lachlan

● Newcastle

Great Dividing Range

★ Sydney

★ Adelaide

Murray

■ CANBERRA (A.C.T.)

▲ Mt. Kosciusko 7,310 ft.

VICTORIA

★ Melbourne

Bass Strait

N

TASMANIA

★ Hobart

0   250   500   750   Kilometers
0 100 200 300 400 500 Miles

Geography

The wettest, most fertile areas of Australia are concentrated along the coastline. The northern coast is tropical and humid, with lush rain forests and mangrove swamps. The fertile strip along the east and southeast coasts rises to the rocky Great Dividing Range. The highest peaks of this range are known as the Australian Alps.

West of the Great Dividing Range lie vast plains broken by occasional rocky hills. The landscape includes scrub, sparse pasture, and dried-out river beds. Water from wells enables livestock to be grazed there. Beyond these plains a huge plateau covers the western two thirds of Australia. Much of this interior is a baking wilderness of stone and cracked clay. However, the southwest coast enjoys warm dry summers and moist winters. The mountainous island of Tasmania lies southeast of the mainland.

Economy

Most of Australia's wealth has come from farming and mining. Although much of the country is too dry for growing crops, the vast grasslands are ideal for grazing large numbers of sheep and cattle. Crops such as wheat, sugarcane, and fruit are grown on only about five percent of the farmland, but this land is highly productive because of modern farming methods. Australia's major farming exports include wool, meat, and dairy products, as well as wines made from grapes grown in the south.

Since the 1800s Australia has exported large amounts of minerals, including gold, copper, silver, and zinc. Huge deposits of bauxite (used to make aluminum), iron ore, and coal were discovered in the 1950s and oil and gas were found in the 1960s. Today a larger part of the Australian work force is employed in service industries.

Boomerang and shield
● ● ● ● ● ● ● ● ● ● ● ● ● ● ●

Aboriginals have used boomerangs for hunting for thousands of years. If thrown properly, a boomerang will come back. The boomerang and shield are made of decorated wood.

Surfing
● ●

Surfing is one of Australia's most popular sports. For outdoor pursuits, Australians wear sunscreen cream to protect their skin against burning in the fierce sun.

People

The Aboriginals were the first people to live in Australia. The word aboriginal means, "there in the beginning." The Aboriginals lived a nomadic life, hunting and gathering food wherever they went. Today only one and a half percent of Australians belong to this ethnic group and very few follow the traditional way of life. In recent years some Aboriginals have campaigned successfully for rights to the land that was taken from them by European settlers.

Most Australians originally came from Europe. By far the greatest proportion came from Britain and Ireland, but large numbers of Greeks, Italians, and Slavs also settled here. Since the 1950s the Australian way of life has been enriched by the traditions, customs, and foods of other immigrant groups, including those from Southeast Asia and Japan.

Opals
• • • • • • • • • • • • •

Opals are iridescent stones used in jewelry. The finest opals in the world are mined in northern New South Wales, Australia.

Kangaroo
• •

The kangaroo is a marsupial, a mammal that carries its baby in its pouch. Kangaroos live on grassy plains and move about in troops, springing on their powerful hind legs.

173

ANTARCTICA

Antarctica is the world's fifth continent and its coldest by far. The landscape and climate are so harsh that people have never settled here permanently, and the only inhabitants are visiting scientists who carry out research projects. The first people to cross the Antarctic Circle were probably Maoris from New Zealand. In 1773 the English navigator James Cook also crossed the Antarctic Circle, but he never sighted land. The mainland was first sighted in the early 1800s and the South Pole was finally reached by a Norwegian, Roald Amundsen, in 1911.

Antarctica is not owned by any country. However, it is rich in minerals and fish, so various nations have made claims here. Thirty-eight countries support a treaty signed in 1959 encouraging scientific research and peace in Antarctica. In 1991 mining was banned for 50 years in an effort to keep this wilderness unspoilt and unexploited by people. In recent years scientists working in Antarctica to monitor climatic changes have reported a thinning of the ozone layer here. Ozone is a gas, high in the Earth's atmosphere, that protects life on Earth from harmful ultraviolet rays, which can scorch crops and cause skin cancer. The ozone layer is being destroyed by the use of chemicals such as CFCs.

Emperor penguin

The emperor is one of two species of penguins that nest on the ice shelves of Antarctica. Six other species visit Antarctic waters, but they choose to nest and breed on remote islands.

Icebreaker

Only icebreakers can safely navigate around icebergs. Nine tenths of their bulk is submerged beneath the Antarctic waters.

■ CONTINENTAL FACTS
Area: 5,381,600 sq. mi.
Population: No permanent population
Highest point: Vinson Massif (16,062 ft.)
Ice cover: Ice and snow cover 98% of Antarctica
Average depth of ice: 6,600 ft.
Deepest ice: 4,800 m
Mineral resources: In 1991 commercial mining was banned for 50 years
Living resources: Cod, icefish, krill

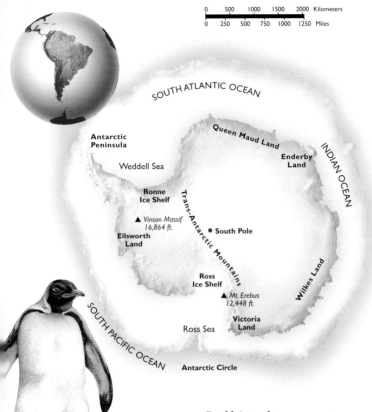

| 0 | 500 | 1000 | 1500 | 2000 Kilometers |
| 0 | 250 | 500 | 750 | 1000 | 1250 Miles |

SOUTH ATLANTIC OCEAN

**Antarctic
Peninsula**

Queen Maud Land

**Enderby
Land**

INDIAN OCEAN

Weddell Sea

**Ronne
Ice Shelf**

Trans-Antarctic Mountains

▲ *Vinson Massif
16,864 ft.*

• **South Pole**

**Ellsworth
Land**

**Ross
Ice Shelf**

Wilkes Land

▲ *Mt. Erebus
12,448 ft.*

**Victoria
Land**

SOUTH PACIFIC OCEAN

Ross Sea

Antarctic Circle

Roald Amundsen

● ●

*The Norwegian explorer, Roald
Amundsen, plants his country's flag at the
South Pole. Amundsen's expedition was
the first to reach the Pole. It arrived on
December 14, 1911.*

THE ARCTIC

The Arctic Circle is an imaginary line around the northern part of the globe. Within this desolate area lies the Arctic Ocean, which is frozen over for much of the year. When the ice breaks up in spring it forms huge floes (fields of ice). Parts of the ocean never melt, but create a great ice cap round the North Pole.

The Arctic Ocean is bordered by Greenland and the northern parts of Canada, Alaska, Russia, and Scandinavia. The people of these snowy lands include the Inuit (Eskimos) of Greenland, North America, and northeast Asia, the Aleuts of Alaska, the Lapps of Scandinavia, and the Yakuts and Chukchee of Russia. Some of them still follow a traditional way of life, hunting fish, seals, and whales, or herding reindeer, which they keep for meat, milk, and hides.

There are many islands in the Arctic, some of them mountainous, and treeless plains called tundra cover a wide area. During the brief summer on the tundra flowers bloom and scrubby plants provide grazing for caribou and reindeer. The Arctic Ocean is rich in plankton, which are devoured by whales. Fish are preyed on by walruses and seals, which in turn are hunted by polar bears.

Russians and Scandinavians explored the Arctic from the 1600s onward, some searching for a sea route around North America to China. The first person to reach the North Pole was Robert Peary of the U.S. Navy in 1909.

■ **THE ARCTIC**
Area (Arctic Ocean): 3,651,800 sq. mi.
Average depth of Ocean: 4,300 ft.
Deepest point: 7,876 ft.
Mineral resources: Oil, natural gas, coal
Living resources: Fish, seals

■ **GREENLAND**
Area: 836,300 sq. mi.
Population: 55,000
Capital: Godthaab (11,000)
Official languages: Danish, Greenlandic
Currency: Danish krone
Main exports: Fish, cryolite, skins

Arctic tern

The Arctic tern breeds on Arctic coasts, then migrates farther than any other bird, to the Antarctic at the other end of the world.

Polar bear

Polar bears live on Arctic coasts. They are strong swimmers. Their fur and fat protect them against the icy waters.

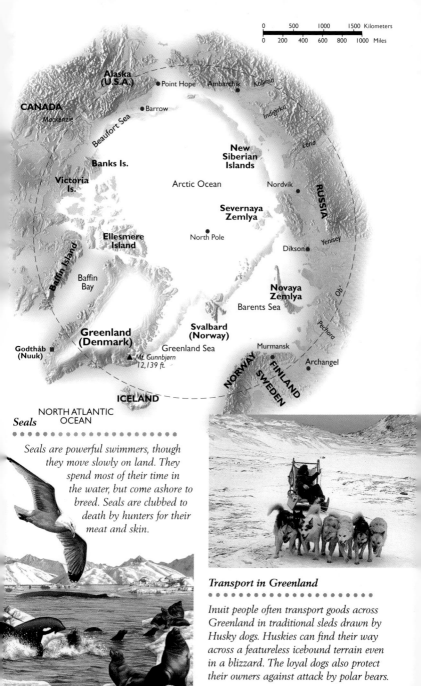

500   1000   1500 Kilometers
200 400 600 800 1000 Miles

Alaska
(U.S.A.)
Point Hope   Ambarchik   Kolyma

CANADA
Mackenzie
Barrow
Beaufort Sea
Indigirka

Banks Is.
New
Siberian
Islands

Arctic Ocean
Nordvik
RUSSIA

Victoria
Is.

Severnaya
Zemlya

Ellesmere
Island
North Pole
Dikson   Yenisey

Baffin Island
Baffin
Bay

Novaya
Zemlya
Barents Sea

Ob

Greenland
(Denmark)
Svalbard
(Norway)
Greenland Sea
Murmansk
Pechora

Godthåb
(Nuuk)
▲ Mt. Gunnbjørn
12,139 ft.
NORWAY   FINLAND
SWEDEN
Archangel

ICELAND

NORTH ATLANTIC
OCEAN

Seals

● ● ● ● ● ● ● ● ● ● ● ● ● ● ● ● ● ●

*Seals are powerful swimmers, though
they move slowly on land. They
spend most of their time in
the water, but come ashore to
breed. Seals are clubbed to
death by hunters for their
meat and skin.*

Transport in Greenland

● ● ● ● ● ● ● ● ● ● ● ● ● ● ● ● ● ● ● ●

*Inuit people often transport goods across
Greenland in traditional sleds drawn by
Husky dogs. Huskies can find their way
across a featureless icebound terrain even
in a blizzard. The loyal dogs also protect
their owners against attack by polar bears.*

177

GLOSSARY

W**ords in italics have their own separate glossary entry.**

Currency is the type of money a country uses, such as rupees in India and dollars in the U.S.A.

■ **Acid rain** Rain that has been made very acidic by waste gases from factories and cars. These gases pollute the atmosphere and also pollute rainfall. Acid rain can cause great damage to plants and animals. It can even damage the surface of buildings.

■ **Agriculture** Using land for growing crops and/or for keeping and grazing animals.

■ **Ancestor** Relative from whom a person is descended, such as a great-great grandparent.

■ **Apartheid** Policy of separating and keeping apart people from different races.

■ **Archipelago** Group of islands.

■ **Atoll** Coral reef or islands that form a partial or complete ring around a *lagoon*.

■ **Atomic bomb** Highly destructive bomb. Its energy comes from splitting tiny chemical particles called atoms.

■ **Bauxite** A raw material used to make aluminum.

■ **Cash crop** Crop grown to sell rather than to feed the grower's own family.

■ **Cassava** Tropical plant with starchy roots. The root is dried and pounded to make flour for bread and tapioca for puddings.

■ **Censorship** System that prevents the communication of certain ideas in words or pictures.

■ **Civil war** War between opposing groups of people within the same country.

■ **Colony** Area taken over or settled by people who have invaded from another country.

■ **Communism** Political system where land, industry, and all property and goods are controlled by the government or *state*.

■ **Copra** Dried coconut kernels from which an oil is extracted.

■ **Currency** Type of money used within a country, such as Indian rupees and U.S. dollars.

■ **Cyclone** Very stormy weather with violent spiralling winds. A tropical cyclone is another name for a *hurricane*.

■ **Deforestation** Loss of areas of forest. Some forests are cut down for their timber. Others may be cleared to make way for buildings or agriculture. In many parts of the world, conservationists are carrying out projects to replace trees and protect forests.

■ **Delta** Area at the mouth of a river where the stream of water divides into several channels, flowing through deposits of sand and mud.

■ **Democracy** System of government where the people have a certain amount of power because they elect those who govern them.

■ **Democratic election** Election that allows the people of a country to choose who governs them. Each person has one vote.

■ **Dependency** Area of land that is controlled or supported by another country.

■ **Descendant** Person who comes from particular *ancestors*. You are a descendant of your great-great-great grandparents.

■ **Dike (or dyke)** Bank or wall built to hold back the sea or a river to prevent flooding. The word is also used for a channel or a ditch dug to drain wet land.

■ **Drought** A long period of dry weather that causes a severe shortage of water.

■ **Economy** The way a country produces, uses, and distributes its goods and services.

■ **Elder** Older person in a community who is greatly respected for knowledge and wisdom gained over a lifetime.

■ **Empire** Group of *colonies* or *territories* that is controlled by a country or power.

Deltas at the mouths of rivers are often shaped like the Greek letter Δ ("D," called delta in Greek). This is how they got their name.

■ **Equator** Imaginary line around the middle of the Earth, at an equal distance from the North and South Poles.

■ **Erosion** Wearing away of rock, land, or buildings by running water, ice, winds, or sea waves.

■ **Ethnic group** Group of people with distinguishing characteristics, such as language, religion, racial origin, or customs.

■ **Exploit** a) To develop land or resources; b) to use land, resources or people for selfish reasons. Colonists in many parts of the world have often got rich by exploiting people and local natural resources.

■ **Export** Product made in one country and sold to another.

■ **Extinct** No longer in existence. Groups of people, animals and plants that have died out and volcanoes that no longer erupt are said to be extinct.

■ **Famine** An extreme shortage of food that may lead to people dying of starvation.

■ **Federal** A system where a nation is divided into several *states*, *provinces*, or *territories*. Each separate area is self-governing in local matters, while a central government decides national matters.

■ **Fjord** Narrow, deep, and steep-sided inlet of the sea in a mountainous area.

■ **Fossil** Remains or evidence of an animal or plant that lived a long time ago. Fossils are usually found hardened in rock.

■ **Free market** Economic system where the government does not control the *economy*.

179

- **Geyser** Natural hot spring that throws up jets of steam or hot water out of the ground.
- **Glacier** Huge mass of ice that moves slowly downhill, along a river valley. Glaciers form high up in the mountains, where the snow piles up year after year.
- **Gorge** Deep, narrow, steep-sided valley.
- **Guerrilla** Member of a group of armed rebels fighting against the controlling force of a country.
- **Habitat** The specific natural surroundings in which animals and plants live.
- **Humid** Moist or damp, as in air or climate.
- **Hurricane** Storm with winds that travel at speeds of more than 70 miles per hour.
- **Hydroelectric power** Electricity made by using the power of water from rivers or lakes that have been dammed.
- **Ice Age** Period of time on a planet when temperatures are extremely low for a very long time. Ice Ages took place on Earth long ago and lasted millions of years. The last one ended around 10,000 years ago.
- **Import** Product that is brought into a country from abroad.
- **Inflation** Overall rise in the price of goods and services. This in turn leads to a fall in the value of money. When money is devalued, it means that more is needed to buy the same goods.
- **Intensive farming** Ways of getting the greatest amount of agricultural produce possible from a piece of land. Intensive farming methods include using

A gorge is a deep, narrow, steep-sided valley. This is Samaria Gorge in Crete.

chemical fertilizers and pesticides and modern farming machinery, as well as rearing large numbers of animals in a small space.
- **Investment** Money that people put into developing a project such as a business or industry.
- **Irrigation** System for providing a supply of water to crops where rainfall is poor.
- **Lagoon** Freshwater or saltwater lake that is separated from the sea by a sandbank or coral reef.
- **Land reclamation** Bringing flooded or wasteland back into use by either draining or clearing.
- **Legislation** The laws of a country and how these laws are drawn up and put into practice.
- **Manufacturing industry** Large-scale factory production of a wide range of goods.
- **Military rule** Government by the armed forces of a country.
- **Mineral** Naturally occurring substance found in the ground. Gold, coal, precious stones, and salt are all minerals. They are valuable *natural resources*.

■ **Monarchy** Land ruled by a king, queen, emperor, or empress. Monarchs have varying degrees of power. In a constitutional monarchy most of the power is held by a *democratically elected* government. A monarch's title is hereditary, which means that it is passed down from one generation to the next.

■ **Monsoon** Extremely strong seasonal wind that can be accompanied by very wet stormy weather. The best-known monsoons occur in southern Asia. They blow from the land to the sea in winter and from the sea to the land in summer.

■ **Multiparty election** Election in which voters can choose between several different political groups or parties.

■ **Native** Person born and living in a particular area.

■ **Natural resource** Part of the natural environment, such as fertile land and minerals, that can be used to produce something else. A work force of people is also a natural resource.

A nomad is someone who regularly moves from place to place in search of food or grazing for animals such as camels or goats. Nomads sleep in tents made of the skin or felted hair of their animals. They live off the meat and milk of their herds and sell the hides.

■ **Navigation** The skill of trying to find the easiest, quickest route from one place to another. The term is used in reference to sea, air, and land travel.

■ **Nomad** Person who regularly moves from place to place in search of food or grazing for animals such as camels, reindeer, sheep, or goats. The land where nomads live is usually not hospitable or fertile enough to support settled communities.

■ **Nuclear power** Energy released by causing reactions to take place within the nuclei (central parts) of atoms. This energy can be produced and used in power stations to provide electricity.

■ **Peninsula** Area of land jutting out from the mainland and surrounded by sea on three sides.

■ **Pesticide** Poison that is used to kill pests and weeds that interfere with crop growing. Many people are looking for alternatives to pesticides, because they can cause a lot of damage to the environment, and sometimes to humans and other animals.

■ **Petrochemical industry** Manufacturing industry using chemicals that are made from crude oil or natural gas. Products of this industry include plastics, fertilizers, and medicines.

■ **Plain** Large area of flat land.

■ **Plantation** Large farm or estate where valuable *cash crops* such as tea, coffee, sugar, or cotton are grown. Just one crop is often grown on a plantation.

■ **Plateau** Large area of flat or fairly flat land that is raised above the surrounding country.

■ **Poaching** Stealing animals from private land. These animals may be prized as food, or for some other valuable product. Many poachers steal animals that are endangered or protected by the law. For example, elephants are killed for their ivory tusks and certain birds and monkeys are stolen so they can be sold as pets.

■ **Pollution** The result of damaging the air, land, or water with harmful substances. These substances include waste products from industry, power stations, cars, and *intensive farming* methods.

■ **Principality** Area of land ruled by a prince. As with a *monarchy*, the ruler may have a small or large amount of real power.

■ **Protectorate** Area of land that is under the protection and partial control of another country.

■ **Province** Area of land that is part of a country or *empire*.

■ **Public spending** The spending of money collected from the people in taxes. The government decides how this will be spent.

■ **Racism** Unfair treatment of one race by another because of unreasonable fear or hatred. As a result people may be insulted or attacked, denied jobs, decent housing, and education.

■ **Raw material** Natural substance that can be made into other products. Iron ore is a raw material used to make steel.

■ **Refinery** Factory where *raw materials* are broken down and processed so that they can be used to make other products. Crude oil is refined to make petroleum and other fuels.

■ **Refugee** Person forced to flee his or her home country. This might be because of war, famine, or religious or political beliefs.

■ **Republic** Country where the people vote for the head of state, who is often the head of the government. The country is usually headed by a president, rather than a monarch. In a democratic republic the people elect their government from a choice of political parties.

■ **Revolution** Overthrow of an existing system of government replacing it with another. Force and violence are frequently used to achieve this.

■ **Riot** Disturbance that involves a crowd of people. A riot may be very violent.

■ **Sanction** Action taken by a government as a way of making a protest against an organization or country. A sanction usually restricts trade and therefore limits income. Several countries might refuse to trade with another country where a certain group of people are being treated very badly. Sanctions are taken in the hope that they will force the country to change its policies.

■ **Savanna** Large grassy region, found in tropical or subtropical areas, where few or no trees grow.

■ **Service industry** Industry providing services for people rather than goods. Tourism, health care, entertainment, education, catering, and banking are all service industries.

■ **Settler** Someone who goes to live permanently in an undeveloped area.

■ **Shaman** Priest or priest-doctor figure found mainly in Asia.

■ **Shanty town** Area of poor, makeshift dwellings, usually on the edge of a town. These areas grow up because there is not enough housing for everyone in the town.

■ **Shrine** Holy place with a special meaning for a certain religious group.

■ **Slash-and-burn agriculture** Growing crops on land that has been cleared by cutting down trees and burning plant life. Land that has been cleared like this does not stay fertile for very long and so the people move on to slash and burn a new plot.

■ **Slavery** Buying and selling of humans, who then become the property of the buyer. Slaves are denied freedom and forced to work without payment.

■ **Sorghum** A kind of grass that produces a nourishing grain used to make bread.

■ **State** Large community that is organized under one local or national government. The word is also used to mean the government of a country, especially a communist country.

■ **Strike** A period when workers stop working to protest against low wages or poor conditions.

■ **Subsidy** Money given by governments to certain industries or organizations to keep prices down or improve production.

■ **Subsistence farming** A method by which farmers can grow only enough food to support themselves and their families, with few or no extra crops to sell.

■ **Territory** When it is used as an official term, territory means an area of land that is controlled by a *state* or country.

■ **Terrorist** Someone who tries to achieve political ends by using violence and intimidation.

■ **Trawling** Method of catching large numbers of fish by dragging a big, wide-mouthed net through the sea.

■ **Tributary** River that flows into another, larger river.

■ **Tsunami** Wave caused by an earthquake on the seabed.

■ **Tundra** Treeless *plain* in the far north that supports mainly mosses, lichens, and small hardy shrubs. The subsoil of the tundra (soil beneath the top layer) is permanently frozen.

■ **Typhoon** Another name for a small violent storm or *cyclone*.

■ **Veld** Large stretch of open grassland found in parts of southern Africa.

Trawling is a common method of catching fish. A net is dragged behind a fishing vessel called a trawler.

INDEX

Page numbers in italic refer to the illustrations and maps

A

Aachen, Germany 69
Aberdeen, Scotland 65
Aboriginals 159, 170, 172, 173
Abu Dhabi, UAE 131, 135
Abuja, Nigeria 144, 146
Accra, Ghana 144, 146
Aconcagua, Mt. 10, 11, 50
Addis Ababa, Ethiopia 139, 140
Adelaide, Australia 171
Aden, Gulf of 153
Aden, Yemen 153
Adriatic Sea 84, 92, 93
Aegean Sea 92, 93
Afar people 153
Afghanistan 124, 125, 126, 127, 128
Africa 54, 136-57, 136-57
Agra, India 124
Ahaggar Mts. 138
Aār Mts. 139
air pollution 14, 15
Al Manamah, Bahrain 131, 135
Alabama 29
Alaska 22, 30, 30, 31
Al'Aziziyah, Libya 10
Albania 92, 94, 94, 95
Albany, NY 29
Alberta, Canada 24
Aleutian Is. 30
Aleuts 176
Alexandria, Egypt 139
Algeciras, Spain 80
Algeria 138, 140, 142, 142
Algiers, Algeria 138, 140
Alicante, Spain 81
Alice Springs, Australia 171
Alkmaar, Netherlands 60
Almaty, Kazakhstan 96, 106
Alps 72, 73, 79
Altai Mts. 105, 110
Altun Mts. 110
Amazon River 10, 40, 46, 47
Amazon basin 49
American Samoa 160, 162, 165
Amiens, France 77
Amin, Idi 148
Amman, Jordan 130, 135
Amritsar, India 124
Amsterdam, Netherlands 61, 62
Amundsen, Roald 174, 175
Amur, River 10
Andes Mts. 40, 42, 50, 51, 52
Andorra 81, 82, 83
Angel Falls, Venezuela 11, 40

Angola 154, 156
Ankara, Turkey 130, 134
Annapurna 11
Antananarivo, Madagascar 155, 156
Antarctica 174, 174-5
Antigua and Barbuda 35, 37
Antilles 39
Antwerp, Belgium 61
apartheid 155
Apia, Western Samoa 165
Appalachian Mts. 29, 30
Arabian Desert 10
Arabian Peninsula 132
Arabs 133, 134, 138
Aral Sea 96
Archangel, Russia 96
archipelagos 122
Arctic 25, 176, 176-7
Arctic Circle 22, 27, 31, 56, 59, 98, 176
Arctic Ocean 24, 57, 176, 177
Ardennes Mts. 61, 62
Argentina 16, 50, 51, 52
Århus, Denmark 57
Arizona 28, 30
Arkansas 29
Armagh, N. Ireland 65
Armenia 96, 103, 106
Arnhem, Netherlands 61
Arnhem Land, Australia 171
Ashgabat, Turkmenistan 96, 107
Asia 54, 108-29, 109-29
Asmera, Eritrea 139, 140
Assal, Lake 136
Asunción, Paraguay 50, 52
Aswan, Egypt 139, 141
Aswan Dam, Egypt 143, 143
Atacama Desert 10, 40, 51
Athabasca Glacier, Canada 27
Athens, Greece 92, 93, 93, 95
Athlone, Ireland 65
Atlanta, GA 29
Atlantic Ocean 58
Atlas Mts. 138, 141
Auckland, N. Zealand 167
Augsburg, Germany 69
Augusta, GA 29
Austin, TX 29
Australasia 158-73, 158
Australia 16, 158, 170-3, 170-3
Australian Desert 10
Austria 72, 73, 74
Avignon, France 77
Avila, Spain 80
Ayers Rock, Australia 171
Azerbaijan 96, 104, 106
Aztecs 35, 38

B

Babylonians 12
Baffin Bay 177
Baffin Is., Canada 11, 25, 26, 177
Baghdad, Iraq 131, 135
Bahamas 35, 36, 39
Bahrain 131, 132, 135
Baikal, Lake 10, 97
Bairiki, Kiribati 164
Baku, Azerbaijan 96, 106
Balaton, Lake 88
Bali, Indonesia 120
Balkans 92-5, 92-4
Balkash, Lake 96
Baltic Sea 57, 70, 89
Baltic States 99, 102
Baltimore, MD 29
Bamako, Mali 138, 140
Bandar Seri Begawan, Brunei 120, 123
Bangkok, Thailand 120, 123
Bangladesh 16, 124, 125, 127, 128
Bangui, Central African Republic 149, 150
Banjul, Gambia 144, 146
Banks Is., Canada 24, 177
Bantry, Ireland 65
Barbados 35, 37
Barcelona, Spain 81
Barents Sea 177
Basel, Switzerland 73
Basque people 82
Bass Strait 171
Basseterre, St. Kitts-Nevis 37
Bastogne, Belgium 61
Baton Rouge, LA 29
Bavarian Alps 68, 70, 71
Beaufort Sea 177
Beijing, China 111, 112
Beirut, Lebanon 130, 134
Belarus 96, 99, 100, 102, 107
Belfast, N. Ireland 65, 66
Belgium 61, 62, 63
Belgrade, Yugoslavia 92, 95
Belize 34, 36
Belmopan, Belize 34, 36
Benelux countries 60
Benguela, Lake 154
Benin 144, 146
Berbers 136, 138
Berchtesgaden, Germany 71
Bergamo, Italy 84
Bergen, Norway 57
Bering Sea 97
Bering Strait 30
Berlin, Germany 69, 70
Berlin Wall 18
Bern, Switzerland 73, 74
Bhutan 124, 127, 129, 129
Bilbao, Spain 81
Bioko 145

Birmingham, England 65
Biscay, Bay of 77
Bishkek, Kyrgyzstan 96, 107
Bismarck, ND 28
Bismarck Archipelago 162
Bissau, Guinea-Bissau 144, 146
Black Forest, Germany 69, 70
Black Sea 92, 103
Bloemfontein, S. Africa 154, 156
Bogotá, Colombia 43, 45
Bohemian Forest, Germany 69
Boise, ID 28
Bokassa, Jean-Bedel 149
Bolívar, Simón 46
Bolivia 42, 43, 45
Bologna, Italy 84, 85
Bolsheviks 98
Bombay, India 124, 125
Bonn, Germany 69
Bordeaux, France 77
Borneo 11, 120
Bosnia-Herzegovina 92, 94, 95
Boston, MA 29
Bothnia, Gulf of 57
Botswana 154, 155, 156
Boulogne, France 77
Boyoma Falls, Zaire 11
Bradford, England 65
Brasília, Brazil 46, 49, 49
Bratislava, Slovak Republic 88
Brazil 16, 43, 46, 47-9
Brazzaville, Congo 144, 147
Breda, Netherlands 61
Bremen, Germany 69
Brest, France 77
Bridgetown, Barbados 37
Brighton, England 65
Brisbane, Australia 171
Bristol, England 65
Britain 11, 54, 65
British Columbia, Canada 24
British empire 126, 128
British Isles 64-7, 65
Brittany 76
Brno, Czech Republic 88
Bruges, Belgium 61
Brunei 120, 121, 123
Brussels, Belgium 61, 62, 63
Bucharest, Romania 92, 95
Budapest, Hungary 88, 91
Buddhism 21, 116, 121, 126, 126
Buenos Aires, Argentina 50, 52
Buffalo, NY 29
Bujumbura, Burundi 149, 150
Bulawayo, Zimbabwe 154
Bulgaria 92, 93, 95
Burkina Faso 144, 146
Burma see Myanmar
Burundi 149, 150, 151
Byzantine empire 109

Cabinda, Angola 148, 154
Cadiz, Spain 80

Cagliari, Italy 84
Cairo, Egypt 139, 140
Calais, France 77
Calama, Chile 10
Calcutta, India 124
Calgary, Canada 24
California 28
Cambodia 120, 121, 123
Cambridge, England 65
Cameroon 144, 147
Canada 16, 22, 24-7, 24-5
Canadian Shield 24, 27
canals 63
Canary Is. 138
Canberra, Australia 170, 170, 171
Cannes, France 77
Cape Horn 50
Cape Town, S. Africa 154, 156
Cape Verde Is. 146
Cape York Peninsula, Australia 171
Caracas, Venezuela 46, 49
Cardiff, Wales 65, 66
Caribbean 22, 34-9, 34-5, 39
Carnival 47, 48
Carpathian Mts. 88, 92
Carpentaria, Gulf of 171
Carson City, NV 28
Cartagena, Spain 81
Casablanca, Morocco 138
Cascade Range 28
Caspian Sea 54, 96, 99, 104, 105, 108
Castries, St. Lucia 36
Catalans 83
cattle 52, 53
Caucasus Mts. 99, 103, 104
Cayenne, French Guiana 46, 49
Cayman Is. 35
Celts 74, 82
censuses, population 17
Central Africa 148-53, 148-53
Central African Republic 148-9, 149, 150
Central America 34-9, 34-5
Chad 139, 140
Chad, Lake 139, 142
Chang Jiang River 10, 108
Channel Is. 65
Charleroi, Belgium 61
Charleston, WV 29
Chartres, France 77
Chechnya, Russia 101
Cherbourg, France 77
Chernobyl, Ukraine 96, 101
Cherrapunji, India 10
Cheyenne, WY 28
Chicago, IL 29, 32
Chile 50, 51, 52
Chimu people 44, 45
China 16, 110-13, 110-13
Chisinau, Moldova 96, 107
Christchurch, N. Zealand 167
Christianity 20, 21
Chukchee people 176
Chuquicamata 53
Churchill, Canada 24

cigars 35
Cincinnati, OH 29
Cleveland, OH 29
climate 10
coffee 38
Coimbra, Portugal 80
Cold War 54, 98
collective farms 114
Cologne, Germany 69, 71
Colombia 42, 43, 45
Colombo, Sri Lanka 124, 127
colonies 136, 144
Colorado 28
Columbia, SC 29
Columbus, OH 29
Commonwealth of Independent States 102
communism 18-19, 89, 90, 94, 100, 108, 114, 115, 115, 121
Comoros 155, 157
Conakry, Guinea 144, 146
Concord, MA 29
Confucianism 20, 21
Congo 144, 147
Connecticut 29
Constance, Lake 69
continental drift 7
Cook, James 174
Copenhagen, Denmark 57, 58
copper 53
coral atolls 160, 164
Coral Sea 160
Córdoba, Spain 80, 83
Cork, Ireland 65
cork oaks 80
Corsica, France 84
Costa Rica 35, 37
Côte d'Ivoire 136, 144, 146
cotton 98, 145
Crete, Greece 92, 93
Croatia 92, 94, 94, 95
Crusaders 132
crust, Earth's 6, 7
Cuba 35, 37, 39
Cyprus 130, 132, 132, 134
Czech Republic 5, 88, 90-1

Dakar, Senegal 144, 146
Dallas, TX 29
Damascus, Syria 130, 134
Danube River 72, 91, 93
Dar-es-Salaam, Tanzania 149
Darling River 158
Darwin, Australia 171
Davis Strait, Canada 25
Dawson, Canada 24
Dead Sea 108
Death Valley, CA/NV 22
deforestation 14-15, 14
Delaware 29
Delhi, India 124, 127
deltas 128, 179
democracy 18, 19, 54, 136
Denmark 56, 57, 58, 59
Denver, CO 28
dependencies 19
Derby, England 65
Des Moines, IA 29
deserts 10, 130, 132, 134,

138, 141
Detroit, MI 29
Dhaka, Bangladesh 124, 127
Dhaulagiri, Nepal 11
diamonds 155, 157
dictatorships 18
Dieppe, France 77
Dijon, France 77
diseases 17
Djibouti 139, 149, 150, 153
Dodoma, Tanzania 149, 150
Doha, Qatar 131, 135
Dominica 35, 37
Dominican Republic 35, 37, 39
Dortmund, Germany 69
Dover, England 65, 67
Dover, DE 29
Drakensberg Mts. 154
Dresden, Germany 69
droughts 141, 142, 153
Dubai, UAE 131
Dublin, Ireland 65, 66
Duisburg, Germany 69
Dundee, Scotland 65
Dunedin, N. Zealand 167
Dunkerque, France 77
Durban, S. Africa 154
Durham, England 65
Dushanbe, Tajikistan 96, 107
Düsseldorf, Germany 69

earthquakes 22, 34, 42, 117, 168
East Africa 148-53, 148-53
Easter Is., Chile 159, 161
Eastern Orthodox Church 20
economics 19
Ecuador 42, 43, 45
Edinburgh, Scotland 65, 66
Edmonton, Canada 24
Egypt 138, 139, 140, 141, 142, 143, 143
Eindhoven, Netherlands 61
El Dorado 45
El Paso, TX 28
El Salvador 34, 37
Elbrus, Mt., Russia 11, 54
elections 18
Ellesmere Is., Canada 11, 24, 177
Ellsworth Land, Antarctica 175
Enderby Land, Antarctica 175
England 64, 65, 66
English Channel 65, 77
Enschede, Netherlands 61
environment 14-15
equator 12
Equatorial Guinea 144, 147
Erie, Lake 25, 29
Eritrea 139, 140
erosion 15
Esbjerg, Denmark 57
Esfahan, Iran 131
Eskimos see Inuit people
Essen, Germany 69
Estonia 96, 102, 106, 107

Ethiopia 138, 139, 140, 141, 142, 143, 153
Europe 54-107, 55
European Union 54, 55, 60, 63, 64, 71, 74, 82, 87
eutrophication 15
Everest, Mt. 11, 108, 110, 124, 129
Exeter, England 65
Eyre, Lake 158, 171

Faeroes 56
Falkland Is. 50
famines 153
federal states 19
Ferrara, Italy 84
Fiji 160, 160, 163, 165
Finland 56, 57, 58, 59
fishing 38, 44, 56, 58, 66, 97, 119, 163, 164, 176, 183
Flemings 63
floods 128
Florence, Italy 84
Flores, Indonesia 120
Florida 29, 31
Fongafale, Tuvalu 165
Fontainebleau, France 77
forests 14-15, 14, 51, 59, 67, 99, 122; see also rain forests
Forth Bridge, Scotland 67
France 76-9, 76-9, 138
Frankfort, KY 29
Frankfurt, Germany 68, 69, 70
Franks 63
Fredericton, Canada 25
free markets 19
Freetown, Sierra Leone 144, 146
French Guiana 46, 47, 48, 49
French Polynesia 161, 165
French Revolution 76
Frisian Is. 61
Frisians 63
fruit 31
Fundy, Bay of 10

Gabon 144, 147
Gaborone, Botswana 156
Galapagos Is. 161
Galicians 82
Galway, Ireland 65
Gambia 144, 146
Gandhi, Mahatma 126
Ganges River 128
gauchos 40, 52
Gdansk, Poland 88
Geneva, Switzerland 73
Genghis Khan 115
Genoa, Italy 84, 85, 87
Georgetown, Guyana 46, 49
Georgia 96, 103, 103, 106
Georgia, USA 29
Germany 18, 68-71, 69-71
geysers 56, 166, 167, 168
Ghana 144, 146
Ghana empire 138, 144
Ghent, Belgium 61

Giant's Causeway, N. Ireland 67
Gibraltar 83
Gibson Desert 171
glaciers 56
Glasgow, Scotland 65
global warming 14
Gobi Desert 10, 110
gods and goddesses 20
Godthaab, Greenland 176, 177
gold 155
Goode's projection 13
Goose Bay, Canada 25
Gorbachev, Mikhail 98
gorges 10, 180
government 18-19
Gozo 85
Gran Chaco 50, 52, 53
Granada, Spain 81
Grand Canyon, AZ 10, 28
Graz, Austria 73
Great Barrier Reef, Australia 171
Great Basin, NV 28
Great Bear Lake, Canada 24
Great Lakes, N. America 22, 30
Great Plains, N. America 27, 28
Great Rift Valley, Africa 152
Great Slave Lake, Canada 24
Greece 20, 54, 92, 93-4, 93, 95, 132
Greenland 11, 22, 56, 59, 176, 177
Greenland Sea 58
Greenwich, England 12, 13
Grenada 35, 37
Grenoble, France 77
Groznyy, Russia 101
Guadeloupe 35
Guajira people 51
Guam 160
Guaraní people 51
Guatemala 34, 36
Guatemala City 34
guerrillas 121
Guinea 144, 146
Guinea Bissau 144, 146
Gulf Stream 56
Guyana 46, 47, 48, 49

Habsburg family 60, 74
The Hague, Netherlands 61
Haifa, Israel 130
Hainan Is., China 111
Haiti 35, 36, 39
Halifax, Canada 25
Halle, Germany 69
Hallstatt, Austria 72
Hamburg, Germany 69
Hammerfest, Norway 57
Hanoi, Vietnam 120, 123
Harare, Zimbabwe 154, 157
Harrisburg, PA 29
Harrison, John 13
Hartford, CT 29
Harz Mts., Germany 69
Havana, Cuba 35, 37

Hawaii 30, *30*, 31, *160*
Hebrides, Scotland 65
Heidelberg, Germany *69*
Helena, MT *28*
Hells Canyon, ID 10
Helsinki, Finland *57*, 58
Himalayas 7, *110*, *124*, 129
Hindu Kush *124*
Hinduism 20, 21, 125, 126, 128
Hiroshima, Japan *116*
Hispaniola 39
Hitler, Adolf 70
Ho Chi Minh City, Vietnam *120*
Hobart, Australia *171*
Hokkaido, Japan *116*
Holland 63
Holy Roman Empire 73, 75
Honduras *35*, 36
Hong Kong *111*, 112, *115*
Honiara, Solomon Is. 165
Honshu, Japan 11, *116*
Houston, TX *29*
Huang He River 10, 108
Huari people 44
Hudson Bay, Canada *25*
Hungary *88*, 90, 91
Huron, Lake *25*, *29*
Hussein, Saddam 130
Hutu people 151
Hyderabad, Pakistan *124*
hydroelectric power 59

Ibadan, Nigeria *144*
Iberian Peninsula 80, 82
Ibiza, Spain *81*
ice *174*, *174*, 176
Ice Age 56
Iceland 56, *56*, 58, 59, *59*
Idaho *28*
Iguaçu Falls *41*, *46*
IJsselmeer, Netherlands *61*
Illinois *29*
Incas 42, 44, 51
India 16, 108, *124*-7, *124-7*
Indian Ocean 129
Indiana *29*
Indianapolis, IN *29*
Indonesia 16, 60, *120*, 122, 123
Indus River 128
Innsbruck, Austria *73*
Inuit 25, 26, 101, *176*, *177*
Inverness, Scotland 65
Ionian Sea 93
Iowa *29*
Iran 130, *130*, *131*, 135
Iraq 130, *131*, 135
Ireland 64, *65*, 66, 67
Irish Sea 65
irrigation 128, 132, *134*
Islam 20, 21, 126, 128, 130, 132, 138
Islamabad, Pakistan *124*, 127
islands 11
Isle of Man 65
Israel *130*, 133, 134, 143
Issa people 153
Italy 84-7, *84-7*

Jackson, MS *29*
Jacksonville, FL *29*
Jaipur, India *124*
Jakarta, Indonesia *120*, 123
Jamaica *35*, 36
James Bay, Canada *25*
Jamuna River 128
Japan 16, 116-19, *116-19*
Java, Indonesia *120*
Jefferson City, MO *29*
Jerez de la Frontera, Spain *80*
Jerusalem, Israel 20, *130*, 134
Jews 133, *133*
Jodhpur, India *124*
Johannesburg, S. Africa *154*
Jordan 108, *130*, 134, *134*, 135
Judaism 20, 21
Jupiter 8, *8*
Jura Mts. 72, *77*, 79
Justinian, Emperor *109*

Kabul, Afghanistan *124*, 127
Kahoolawe, Hawaii *30*
Kalahari Desert 10, *154*
Kamavura people *40*
Kamchatka Peninsula 97
Kampala, Uganda *149*, 150, *151*
Kanchenjunga 11
Kansas *28*, 33
Kansas City, MO *29*
Karachi, Pakistan *124*
Karakum Desert 104
Kariba, Lake *154*
Karlsruhe, Germany *69*
Karlstad, Sweden *57*
Kassel, Germany *69*
Katmandu, Nepal *124*, 127, 129
Kauai, Hawaii *30*
Kazakhstan 16, *96*, *102*, 105, 106, 108
Kemal, Mustafa 132
Kentucky *29*
Kenya *149*, 150, 152
Khant people *109*
Khartoum, Sudan *139*, 140
Kiel Canal 70
Kiev, Ukraine *96*, 107
Kigali, Rwanda *149*, 150
Kikuyu people 152
Kilimanjaro, Mt. 11, 136, *149*, 152
Killarney, Ireland 65
Kingston, Jamaica *35*, 36
Kingstown, St. Vincent and the Grenadines 37
Kinshasa, Zaire *148*, 150
Kiribati *160*, *162*, 164
Kirkuk, Iraq *131*
Kopet Mts. 104
Korean War 114
Koror, Palau 164
Kraków, Poland *88*
Kuala Lumpur, Malaysia *120*, 123
Kunlun Mts. *110*
Kurds 130
Kuwait 130, *131*, 132, 135

Kyoto, Japan *116*
Kyrgyzstan *96*, 106, 107
Kyushu, Japan *116*

La Coruña, Spain *80*
La Paz, Bolivia *43*, *44*, 45
La Rochelle, France *77*
Labrador Sea, Canada *25*
Ladoga, Lake *96*
Lagos, Nigeria *144*
Lahore, Pakistan *124*
Lake District, England 65
lakes 10, 15
Lanai, Hawaii *30*
Land's End, England 65
Lansing, MI *29*
Laos *120*, 121, *121*, 123
Lapland *57*, 58, 59
Lapps 176
Las Vegas, NV *28*
latitude 12-13
Latvia *96*, 102, 107
Le Havre, France *77*
Lebanon *130*, 133, 134
Leeds, England 65
Leiden, Netherlands *61*
Leipzig, Germany *69*
Lena River 10
Lenin 98
León, Spain *80*
Lesotho *154*, 156
Liberia *144*, 146
Libreville, Gabon *144*, 147
Libya *138*, *139*, 140, *141*, 142
Liechtenstein 73, *73*, 74, 75
Liäge, Belgium *61*
life 7, 8, 9
Ligurian Sea *84*
Lille, France *77*
Lillehammer, Norway *57*
Lilongwe, Malawi *154*, 156
Lima, Peru *43*, 45
Limerick, Ireland 65
Lincoln, NE *29*
Linköping, Sweden *57*
Lisbon, Portugal *80*, 82, *82*
lithosphere 7, *7*
Lithuania *96*, 102, *103*, 107
Little Rock, AR *29*
Liverpool, England 65
Livingstone, Dr. David *137*
Ljubljana, Slovenia *92*, 95
Lódź, Poland *88*
Logan, Mt., Canada *24*
Lomé, Togo *144*, 146
London, England 53, *64*, 65, 66
Londonderry, N. Ireland 65
longitude 12-13
Los Angeles, CA *28*
Louisiana *29*
Low Countries 60
Luanda, Angola *154*, 156
Lucknow, India *124*
Lusaka, Zambia *154*, 157
Luxembourg 60, *61*, 62, 63
Luxembourg City *61*, 62, 63
Luxor, Egypt *139*
Luzon, Philippines *120*, 122
Lyon, France *77*

187

Maastricht, Netherlands 61
Macao 111, 112, 115
Macedonia 92, 93, 95
Mackenzie River 22
Madagascar 11, 155, 156
Madison, WI 29
Madras, India 124
Madrid, Spain 81, 82
Maine 29
Majuro, Marshall Is. 164
Makalu, Mt., Nepal 11
Makonde people 152
Malabo, Equatorial Guinea 147
Málaga, Spain 80
Malawi 137, 154, 156
Malaysia 120, 122, 123
Maldives 127, 129
Male, Maldives 127
Mali 138, 140, 141
Mali empire 138, 144
Mallorca, Spain 81
Malmö, Sweden 57
Malta 84, 85, 87, 87
Managua, Nicaragua 35, 36
Manchester, England 65
Mandalay, Myanmar 125
Mandela, Nelson 136, 155
Manila, Philippines 120, 123
Manitoba, Canada 24
mantle, Earth's 6-7, 7
Maoris 158, 166, 168, 169, 174
map-making 12-13, 12-13
Maputo, Mozambique 154, 156
Maracaibo, Lake 40, 48
Marbella, Spain 80
Marcos, President 122
Marianas Trench, Pacific Ocean 10
Marrakech, Morocco 138
Mars 8, 8
Marseille, France 77
Marsh Arabs 130
Marshall Is. 160, 163, 164
Martinique 35
Maryland 29
Masai people 148, 152
Maseru, Lesotho 156
Massachusetts 29
Matterhorn 75
Maui, Hawaii 30
Mauritania 138, 140, 142
Mauritius 156, 157
Mayans 34-5
Mbabane, Swaziland 154, 156
Mbini, Equatorial Guinea 144
McKinley, (Denali), AK 11, 22
Mecca, Saudi Arabia 130
Medicine Hat, Canada 24
Mediterranean Sea 77, 79, 84, 87, 143
Mekong River 10
Melanesians 160
Melbourne, Australia 171
Memphis, TN 29
Menorca, Spain 81
Mercator's projection 12, 13

Mercury 8, 8
mestizos 35
Meuse River 63
Mexico 34, 36, 38
Mexico, Gulf of 29
Mexico City 34, 36
Miami, FL 29
Michigan, Lake 29
Michigan 29
Micronesia 160, 160, 164, 164
Middle East 130-5, 130-5
Midway Is. 160
Milan, Italy 84, 85, 87
Milwaukee, WI 29
Mindanao, Philippines 120
mining 142, 157, 172, 174
Minneapolis, MN 29
Minnesota 29
Minsk, Belarus 96, 100, 107
Mississippi 29
Mississippi River 10, 22, 30
Missouri 29
Missouri River 10, 22, 30
Modena, Italy 84
Mogadishu, Somalia 149, 150
Moldova 96, 99, 101, 102, 107
Molokai, Hawaii 30
Mombasa, Kenya 149
Monaco 77, 78, 78
monarchy 19
Mongolia 110, 112, 114, 115
Mongols 108
Monrovia, Liberia 144, 146
Mons, Belgium 61
monsoon 121
Mont Blanc 11
Montana 28
Montevideo, Uruguay 50, 51, 52
Montgomery, AL 29
Montpelier, VT 29
Montpellier, France 77
Montreal, Canada 25, 25
Monument Valley 32
Moon 6
Moors 82
Morocco 136, 138, 138, 140, 142
Moroni, Comoros 157
Moscow, Russia 96, 101, 106
Moselle River 62
Mosul, Iraq 131
mountains 11
Mozambique 154, 156
Munich, Germany 69
Murcia, Spain 81
Murray River 158
Muscat, Oman 131, 132, 135
Muslims see Islam
Mussolini, Benito 86
Myanmar 125, 126, 127, 128
Myvatn, Lake 59

Nagasaki, Japan 116
Nagorno-Karabakh 104
Nairobi, Kenya 149, 150, 152
Namib Desert 157
Namibia 154, 157

Namur, Belgium 61
Nancy, France 77
Nanga Parbat, India 11
Nantes, France 77
Naples, Italy 84
Narvik, Norway 57
Nashville, TN 29
Nassau, Bahamas 35, 36
Native Americans 22, 32, 38, 40, 42-3, 44-5, 47, 48, 51
Nauru 158, 160, 163, 165
navigation 12-13
Nazis 70, 89
N'Djamena, Chad 139, 140
Nebraska 28
nebulae 6
Nepal 124, 127, 128, 129
Neptune 8, 9
Netherlands 54, 60, 61, 62, 62, 63
Netherlands Antilles 35
Nevada 28
New Brunswick, Canada 25
New Caledonia 160, 160, 164
New Guinea 11, 158, 162
New Hampshire 29
New Jersey 29
New Mexico 28
New Orleans, LA 29
New Siberian Is. 177
New South Wales, Australia 171
New York City, NY 29, 33
New York State 29
New Zealand 158, 160, 166-9, 166-9
Newcastle, England 65
Newfoundland, Canada 25
Ngorongoro Crater 152
Niagara Falls 11
Niamey, Niger 138, 140
Nicaragua 35, 36, 38
Nice, France 77
Nicosia, Cyprus 130, 134
Niger 139, 140, 142
Niger River 10, 136
Nigeria 16, 144, 144, 146
Niihau, Hawaii 30
Nijmegen, Netherlands 61
Nile River 10, 136, 138, 141, 143, 143
nomads 59, 105, 106, 126, 141, 153, 173, 181
North Africa 138-43, 138-43
North America 22-33, 23-33, 54, 59
North Carolina 29
North Dakota 28
North Korea 111, 112, 114, 115
North Pole 14, 176, 177
North Sea 58, 59, 70
Northern Ireland 64, 65, 66, 67
Northern Mariana Is. 160
Northern Territories, Canada 24
Northern Territory, Australia 171
Norway 56, 57, 58

Norwich, England 65
Nottingham, England 65
Nouakchott, Mauritania 138, 140
Noumea, New Caledonia 164
Nova Scotia, Canada 25, 26
Novaya Zemlya 177
nuclear waste 15
Nukualofa, Tonga 165
Nunavut 26
Nuremberg, Germany 69
Nyasa, Lake 154

Oahu, Hawaii 30
oases 141
Ob River 10, 108
oceans 10
Odense, Denmark 57
Ohio 29
Ohio River 30
oil 42, 44, 48, 58, 59, 121, 130, 132, 142, 144
Okavango Swamp 154
Okhotsk, Sea of 97
Oklahoma 28
Oklahoma City, OK 29
Olympia, WA 28
Olympus, Mt., Greece 20
Oman 131, 132, 132, 135
Ontario, Canada 25
Ontario, Lake 25, 29
Oregon 28
Orkney Is., Scotland 65
Orleans, France 77
Osaka, Japan 116
Oslo, Norway 57, 58
Ostend, Belgium 61
Ottawa, Canada 24, 25
Ottoman empire 132
Ouagadougou, Burkina Faso 144, 146
Oviedo, Spain 80
Oxford, England 65
ozone layer 14, 174

Pacific Is. 158, 160-5, 160-5
Pacific Ocean 10, 119
Padua, Italy 84
Pago Pago, American Samoa 165
Pakistan 16, 124, 126, 127, 128
Palau 164
Palermo, Italy 84
Palestine 133
Palikir, Micronesia 164
Palma, Mallorca 81
Pamir Mts. 105
Pampas 40, 50, 52
Pamplona, Spain 81
Panama 35, 36
Panama Canal 39
Panama City 35, 36
Papeete, French Polynesia 165
Papua New Guinea 158, 160, 162, 165
Paraguay 50, 51, 52, 53
Paramaribo, Suriname 46, 49
Paris, France 76, 76, 77, 78
Parma, Italy 84

Patagonia 50, 52
Peace River 22, 24
Peary, Robert 176
Peloponnesus 92
Pennines, England 65
Pennsylvania 29
Perth, Australia 170
Peru 42, 43, 44, 45
Perugia, Italy 84
Peters' projection 13
Philadelphia, PA 29
Philippines 120, 122, 122, 123
Phnom Penh, Cambodia 120, 123
Phoenix, AZ 28
phosphates 163
Pierre, SD 28
Pisa, Italy 84, 86
Pitcairn Is. 161
Pittsburgh, PA 29
Pizarro, Francisco 44
planets 6-9, 7-9
Pluto 8, 9
Plymouth, England 65
Poland 88-90, 89, 91
polders 62
pollution 14, 15, 130
Polynesia 159, 160
population 16-17
Port-au-Prince, Haiti 35, 36
Port Louis, Mauritius 156
Port Moresby, Papua New Guinea 160, 165
Port-of-Spain, Trinidad and Tobago 36
Port-Vila, Vanuatu 165
Portland, OR 28
Porto-Novo, Benin 144, 146
Portsmouth, England 65
Portugal 80-2, 80, 82-3
Poznan, Poland 88
Prague, Czech Republic 88, 91, 91
Praia, Cape Verde Is. 146
prairies 31
Pretoria, S. Africa 154, 156
Prince Albert, Canada 24
Prince Edward Is., Canada 25
Prince Rupert, Canada 24
Protestant churches 20
Provence, France 79
Providence, RI 29
Puerto Rico 35, 37, 39
Pyongyang, N. Korea 111, 112
Pyrenees 77, 79, 80, 81

Qatar 131, 132, 135
Quebec, Canada 25, 26
Queen Maud Land, Antarctica 175
Queensland, Australia 171
Quito, Ecuador 43, 45

Rabat, Morocco 138, 140
rainfall 10
rainforests 40, 42, 43, 47, 49, 129, 147, 148, 172
Rainier, Mt., WA 10
Raleigh, NC 29

Ravenna, Italy 84
recycling 15
Red Rock River 22
Red Sea 139, 153
refugees 152
Regensburg, Germany 69
Regina, Canada 24
Reims, France 77
religion 20-1
Renaissance 86
republics 19
Reykjavik, Iceland 56, 58
Rhine River 68
Rhode Island 29
Rhodes, Greece 92
rice 121, 122, 128
Richmond, VA 29
Riga, Latvia 96, 107
Rigestan Desert 124
Rimini, Italy 84
Ring of Fire 122
Rio de Janeiro, Brazil 46, 47
rivers 10, 15
Riyadh, Saudi Arabia 131, 135
Robson, Mt., Canada 24
Rocky Mts., N. America 22, 24, 27, 27, 28, 30
Roman Catholic Church 20, 86
Romania 92, 95
Romans 74, 75, 78, 86
Romany gypsies 82
Rome, Italy 84, 87
Ronda, Spain 80
Roseau, Dominica 37
Ross Ice Shelf, Antarctica 175
Ross Sea 175
Rotterdam, Netherlands 61
Rouen, France 77
Ruhr River 70
Russia 16, 54, 59, 96-101, 96-9, 106
Rwanda 148, 149, 150, 151

Saarbrücken, Germany 69
Sacramento, CA 28
Sahara Desert 10, 138, 138-9, 141
Sahel 141
St. George's, Grenada 37
St. John, Canada 25
St. John's, Antigua and Barbuda 37
St. Kitts-Nevis 22, 35, 37
St. Louis, MO 29
St. Lucia 35, 36
St. Paul, MN 29
St. Petersburg, Russia 96
St. Vincent and the Grenadines 35, 37
Salem, OR 28
salt 129
Salt Lake City, UT 28
Salzburg, Austria 73
Sami people 58, 59
Samoa 160
samurai 119
San Antonio, TX 28
San Diego, CA 28

San Francisco, CA *28*
San Ignacio *53*
San José, Costa Rica *35*, 37
San Jose, CA *28*
San Juan, Puerto Rico *35*, 37
San Marino 85, 87
San people *155*
San Salvador, El Salvador *34*, 37
San Sebastián, Spain *81*
Sana, Yemen *131*, 135
Sandinistas 38
Santa Fe, NM *28*
Santander, Spain *81*
Santiago, Chile *50*, 52
Santiago de Compostela, Spain *80*
Santo Domingo, Dominican Republic *35*, 37
São Tomé and Príncipe *144*, 147
Sarajevo, Bosnia-Herzegovina *92*, 95
Sardinia, Italy *84*
Saskatchewan, Canada *24*
Saskatoon, Canada *24*
Saturn 8, *9*
Saudi Arabia *131*, 132, 135, 153
Sauer River 62
savanna *147*, 148
Saxons 63
Scandinavia 56-9, *57*
Schelde River 63
Schellenberg, Liechtenstein 73
Scotland 64, *65*, 66
Search for Extra-Terrestrial Intelligence (SETI) 9
Seattle, WA *28*
Selous Wildlife Reserve 152
Senegal *144*, 146
Seoul, S. Korea *111*, 112
Serbia 94
Serengeti Plain 152
Severnaya Zemlya *177*
Seville, Spain *80*
Seychelles 156
Shanghai, China *111*
Sheffield, England *65*
Shetland Is., Scotland *65*
Shi Huangdi, Emperor *113*
Shikoku, Japan *116*
Shintoism 21
shipbuilding 58
Siberia, Russia *97*, 98, 102, *109*
Sicily, Italy *84*, 85
Sierra Leone *144*, 146
Sikhism 21
Simpson Desert *171*
Singapore *120*, *121*, 123
Skopje, Macedonia *92*, 95
slavery 32, 39, 144
Slovakia *88*, 91
Slovenia *92*, 95
snow 10
Sofia, Bulgaria *92*, 95
soil erosion 15
Solar System 8-9, *8-9*

Solidarity 89
Solomon Is. *160*, 162, 165
Somalia *139*, *149*, 150, 152, 153, *153*
Somoza, Anastasio 38
Songhai empire 138, 144
South Africa 136, *154*, 155, 155, 156, 157
South America 40-53, *41-53*, 54
South Carolina *29*
South China Sea *120*
South Dakota *28*
Southeast Asia *120-3*
South Georgia *50*
South Korea *111*, 112, 114
South Pole 14, *174*, *175*
Southampton, England *65*
Southern Africa 154-7, *154-7*
Southern Alps *167*, 168
Soviet Union 5, 54, 90, 98, 100, 102, 104, 105, 108, 126
space industry *27*, *29*, *47*
Spain 44-5, 51, 54, 80-3, *80-3*
Sri Lanka *124*, 127, 129
Srinagar, India *124*
Stalin, Joseph 98
stars, navigation 12-13
Stavanger, Norway *57*
steppes 99, 105
Stewart Is., N. Zealand *167*
Stockholm, Sweden 57, 58
Stonehenge, England *64*
Strasbourg, France 77
Stuttgart, Germany 69
Sucre, Bolivia *43*, 45
Sudan 16, 138, *139*, 140, *141*, *143*
Suez, Egypt *139*
Suez Canal 143
Sulawesi *120*
Sulu Sea *120*
Sumatra 11, *120*
Sun 6, 7, 8, 12-13
Superior, Lake 22, *25*, *29*
Suriname *46*, 47, 48, 49
Surtsey 56
Suva, Fiji 165
Swansea, Wales *65*
Swaziland *154*, 156, 157
Sweden 56, *57*, 58, 59
Switzerland 72, 73, 74, 75
Sydney, Australia *171*, 173
Syria *130*, *132*, 133, 134

Tahiti, French Polynesia 165
Taipei, Taiwan *111*, 112
taiga 99
Taiwan *111*, 112, 114
Tajikistan *96*, *104*, *105*, 107
Taklimakan Desert *110*
Tallahassee, FL *29*
Tallinn, Estonia *96*, 107
Tampere, Finland *57*
Tanganyika, Lake *149*
Tangier, Morocco *138*
Tanzania *149*, 150, 152, *152*
Tarragona, Spain *81*
Tashkent, Uzbekistan *96*,

104, 107.
Tasman Sea *160*, *167*
Tasmania, Australia *171*, 172
Tbilisi, Georgia *96*, 106
Tegucigalpa, Honduras *35*, 36.
Tehran, Iran *131*, 135
Tel Aviv, Israel *130*
temperatures 10
Tennessee *29*
Tenochtitlan 38
Texas *28*
Thailand *120*, 121, 123
Thar Desert *124*
Thimphu, Bhutan *124*, 127
Tian Shan Mts. 105
Tibesti Mts., Chad *139*
Tibetan Plateau, China *110*
Tierra del Fuego *50*
Tilburg, Netherlands *61*
Timbuktu, Mali *138*
Timor, Indonesia *120*
Tipperary, Ireland *65*
Tirane, Albania *92*, 95
Tirol, Austria *74*
Titicaca, Lake 10, *42*, *43*
Togo *144*, 146, *147*
Tokyo, Japan *116*, *117*, *118*, *119*
Toledo, Spain *81*
Toledo, OH *29*
Tonga *160*, 165
Topeka, KS *29*
Toronto, Canada *25*, *27*
Torrens, Lake *171*
Toulouse, France 77
tourism 39, 53, 121, 125, 129, 142, 152, 163, 168
Tours, France 77
Transylvanian Alps *92*
Trenton, NJ *29*
Trieste, Italy *84*, 87
Trinidad and Tobago *35*, 36, 39
Tripoli, Libya *139*, 140, *141*
Tromso, Norway *57*
Trondheim, Norway *57*
tsunamis 119
Tuareg 141
Tugela Falls, S. Africa 11
tundra 99, 176
Tunis, Tunisia *139*, 140
Tunisia *139*, 140, 142, *142*
Turin, Italy *84*, 85
Turkana, Lake *149*
Turkey *130*, 132, *133*, 134
Turkmenistan *96*, *104*, *105*, 107
Turks and Caicos Is. *35*
Turku, Finland *57*
Tutsi people 151, *151*
Tutunendo, Colombia 10
Tuvalu *160*, 164, 165
Tyrrhenian Sea *84*

Udine, Italy *84*
Uganda 148, *149*, 150, *151*
Ukraine *96*, 99, *101*, 102, 107
Ulan Bator, Mongolia *110*, 112
United Arab Emirates *131*, 132, 135

United Kingdom 64, 66-7
United Nations (UN) 17, *18*, 19, 75, 130
United States of America 16, 22, 28-33, *28-9*, 54
Uppsala, Sweden 57
Ural Mts. *96*, 99
Uranus 8, *9*
Uru people *42*
Uruguay *50*, 52, 53
Utah *28*
Uzbekistan *96*, 99, *104*, 105, 107, 108

vaccination 17
Vaduz, Liechtenstein 73, *73*, *74*
Valencia, Spain *81*
Valladolid, Spain *80*
Valletta, Malta *84*, 87
Vancouver, Canada *24*
Vancouver Is., Canada *24*
Vänern, Lake 57
Vanuatu 160, *160*, 165
Vatican City 54, 85, 87
Venezuela *46*, 48, 49
Venice, Italy *84*, *85*
Venus 8, *8*
Vermont *29*
Verona, Italy *84*
Victoria, Australia *171*
Victoria, Canada *24*
Victoria, Seychelles 156
Victoria, Lake 136, *149*
Victoria Is., Canada 11, *24*, *177*
Victoria Land, Antarctica *175*
Vienna, Austria *73*, 74, 75
Vienna Basin, Austria 72
Vientiane, Laos *120*, 123
Vietnam *120*, 121, 123
Vietnam War 121
Vigo, Spain *80*
Vikings 59
Vilnius, Lithuania *96*, 107
Vinson Massif, Antarctica 11, *174*, *175*
Virginia *29*
Vladivostok, Russia *97*
volcanoes 34, 42, 56, 59, *117*, 119, 122, 152, 160, *166*, 168
Volga River 54
Vosges Mts. 79
Vostock, Antarctica 10

Wake Is. *160*
Wales 64, *65*, 66
Walloons 63
Waorami people 43
Warsaw, Poland *88*, *90*, 91
Washington, Mt. 10
Washington D.C. *29*, *29*, *31*
Washington State *28*
waterfalls 11, 119, 147
Waterford, Ireland 65
Weddell Sea *175*
Wellington, N. Zealand 166, *167*, 169, *169*
West Africa 144-7, *144-7*

West Indies 39
West Virginia *29*
Western Sahara *138*, 140
Western Samoa *160*, 165
wetlands 15
wheat *31*, 33, 99
Whitehorse, Canada *24*
Wiesbaden, Germany 69
Wilhelm, Mt. 11, 158
Wilkes Land, Antarctica *175*
Windhoek, Namibia *154*, 157
windmills 62
winds 10
wine *61*
Winnipeg, Canada *24*
Winnipeg, Lake *24*
Winston-Salem, NC *29*
Wisconsin *29*
World Health Organization (WHO) 16-17
World War I 54, 64, 70
World War II 54, 64, 70, 71, 89, 119
Wroclaw, Poland *88*
Wuppertal, Germany 69
Wyoming *28*

Yaka people *149*
Yakut people *109*, 176
Yakutsk, Russia *97*
Yamoussoukro, Côte d'Ivoire *144*, 146
Yangon, Myanmar *125*, *126*, 127
Yaoundé, Cameroon *144*, 147
Yaren, Nauru 165
Yellow Sea *111*
Yellowknife, Canada *24*
Yemen *130*, *131*, 132, 135
Yenisey River 10, 108
Yerevan, Armenia *96*, 106
Yokohama, Japan *116*
Yosemite Falls 11
Yugoslavia 5, *92*, 93, 94, 95
Yukon Territory, Canada *24*

Zagreb, Croatia *92*, 95
Zaire *137*, 148, *149*, 150, 151
Zaire River 10, 136, 148
Zambia *154*, 157
Zimbabwe *154*, 157
Zugspitze 70
Zurich, Switzerland *73*

ACKNOWLEDGMENTS

The publishers would like to thank the following sources for providing photographs: PAGE 10/11 (TR) © 1996 Corel Corp.; 15 (BR) David Woodfall/Tony Stone Images; 18 (C) Christopher Morris/Black Star!Colorific!; 19 (BR) Alexandra Avakin/Woodfin Camp World/Telegraph Colour Library; 20 (TR) John Lawrence/ Tony Stone Images; 21 (BR) Hugh Sitton/Tony Stone Images; 21 (BR) Alan Kearney/Tony Stone Images; 26 (BR) Steffan Widstrand/Bruce Coleman Ltd.; 27 (TR) Canadian Tourist Office; 28 (BL) ZEFA; 31 (CR) ZEFA; 32/3 (C) Robert Frerck/Tony Stone Worldwide; 38 (TR) David Hiser/Tony Stone Worldwide; 39 (CR) John Adriaan/Tony Stone Worldwide; 39 (B) Sarah Stone/Tony Stone; 41 (TL) Spectrum Colour Library; 44 (CL) Ingrid Morato/Panos Pictures; 44 (BR) © Tayacan/Panos Pictures; 47 (TR) Guyana Space Centre/South American Pictures; 49 (TL) ZEFA; 53 (TR) M.Barlow/Trip; 53 (L) Julio Etchart/Panos Pictures; 54 (TR) Corbis; 58 (BR) Finnish Tourist Board; 59 (TL) © Goran Assner/Swedish Travel & Tourism Council; 63 (TL) Walter Rawlings/Robert Harding Picture Library; 63 (TR) ZEFA; 67 (CR) Dennis Gilbert/Larousse; 67 (CL) ZEFA; 70 (TR) Ed Pritchard/Tony Stone Worldwide; 71 (B) Robert Harding Picture Library; 72 (TR) Andy Price/Bruce Coleman Ltd.; 73 (BR) Robert Harding Picture Library; 74 (B) Fred Frieberg/Robert Harding Picture Library; 75 (TR) Adam Woolfitt/Robert Harding Picture Library; 75 (TR) Bill O'Connor/Robert Harding Picture Library; 76 (TR) Walter Rawlings/Robert Harding Picture Library; 78 (CL) ZEFA; 79 (T) ZEFA; 81 (BR) Robert Harding Picture Library; 83 (TR) Sean Egan/Tony Stone Images; 83 (TC) Robert Everts/Tony Stone Worldwide; 85 (TR) J. Allan Cash; 85 (B) Jean-Leo Dugast/Panos Pictures; 87 (B) World Pictures/Feature Pix; 88 (BR) Corbis; 90 (BL) Corbis; 90/l (CT) Joe Cornish/Tony Stone Worldwide; 92 (B) George Grigoriou/Tony Stone Images;96 (BL) Liam Muir; 98 (BL) Corbis; 99(TL) Corbis; l00 (TL) A.Boulat/Sipa Press/Rex Features; 10l (BR) V.Shuba/Trip; 104 (TC) Ben Aris/Panos Pictures; 106 (TL) Lehtikuvoy/Rex Features; 113 (TL) Spectrum Colour Library; 113 (C) Julian Calder/Tony Stone Worldwide; 114/5 (T) ZEFA; 115 (BR) ZEFA; 117 (TR) © 1996 Corel Corp; 118 (B) Paul Chesley/Tony Stone Images; 121 (TR) Robert McLeod/Robert Harding Picture Library; 122-l34 all photographs from Corbis; l37 (BR) Andrew Hill/The Hutchison Library; l43 (TL) Christine Osborne Pictures; l43 (BR) Thierry Borredon/Tony Stone Images; l49 (C) HornimanMuseum/Bridgeman Art Library; 153 (BL) Howard Davies/Panos Pictures; 162/3 (C) Tony Stone Worldwide; 164 (BL) Paul Chesley/Tony Stone Worldwide; 168/9 (TC) Robert Harding Picture Library; 171 (TL) Corbis; 173 (TR) Corbis; 174 © Fotex/Drewer/Rex Features; 177 both photographs Rex Features.